PRAYER
Conversing With God

SPECIAL YOUTH EDITION

PRAYER
Conversing With God

by
ROSALIND RINKER

"I never thought of prayer like this."
"Now I can pray to Jesus and not be afraid of what others think."
"It made me feel loved."

ZONDERVAN
PUBLISHING HOUSE

OF THE ZONDERVAN CORPORATION
GRAND RAPIDS, MICHIGAN 49506

PRAYER — CONVERSING WITH GOD
special youth edition
Copyright 1959, 1970 by
Zondervan Publishing House
Grand Rapids, Michigan

Eleventh printing   1977
ISBN 0-310-32101-8

Printed in the United States of America

To
MY MOTHER
who led me to Christ

Contents

Preface

I have discovered that the real purpose of prayer is to concentrate on God at the very center of one's being.

Jesus said, "When thou prayest . . . enter into thy closet and shut the door." Whether we are alone or with others, we must try to forget ourselves and any impression we are making.

This book is autobiographical. In no other way am I able to describe the intimate experiences through which God led me, as I learned to pray conversationally. Actually, the title might well be, "Where two or three agree," from Matthew 18:19, 20 — for this book is based largely on the meaning and content of these well-known verses.

Over a period of more than 25 years of my Christian life, I struggled with many hindrances to effective prayer. I eventually found that the very things that troubled me were the stepping-stones to the new and wonderful lessons God had for me.

Working with various groups, I witnessed the vital response through the simplicity of conversational prayer, transforming and lighting up the true meaning of prayer. I recall one group that spent most of their time singing and giving requests, with only five minutes of prayer. They began to pray conversationally, and the procedure was completely reversed. With joyful astonishment they found they wanted to spend a whole hour praying together!

Praying conversationally, i.e., praying back and forth on a single subject, makes prayer such a natural means of "spiritual togetherness." The healing love of God touches each one of us, because we are in His presence. We realize joyfully what it means to be consciously with Him — brothers and sisters in Christ.

My deep appreciation goes out to all those who encouraged and helped me in my search for reality. To the missionaries with whom I worked in China, to the staff and students of Inter-Varsity Christian Fellowship, and to the pastors and laymen in the churches where I've spoken . . . . for the privilege of testing the material in this book, I am grateful.

I am particularly thankful to Eugenia Price, with whom I was associated, for her encouragement to write, and her assistance with the manuscript in this great adventure with God.

Why a Special Youth Edition?

Because of the many young people I've met in my travels who would like a book of their own. This book was first printed in 1959; since then my three later books on prayer have contained many workable ideas and suggestions in starting groups, or in changing from old prayer-patterns to new. Some of those ideas are now included in Part II of this edition.

Part I. The original chapters are here. With a complete revision of the text — thanks to my good friend, William H. Ward, who assisted in removing awkward coloquialisms which seemed to creep into that first edition.

Part II. The introduction contains an article on dialogue-prayer written and used by John and Vel Shearer in teaching their teens; and a report of my first workshops with those teens, including their reactions. Simplified instructions are given which any teenager may follow with definite results.

ROSALIND RINKER

Revised Edition 1970
Chicago, Illinois.

PART I

The Story
of how
it all began.

CHAPTER 1

Three Prayer Meetings

The first one

For the first fifteen years of my Christian life, I played follow-the-leader where prayer was concerned. In my desire to be a true disciple of Jesus Christ, I somehow found myself following others instead of following Him.

My Christian life began when I was a sophomore in high school. Mother took me to a youth conference where I gave my heart and my life to Jesus Christ. In the next chapter I shall tell you what happened when I unconsciously began imitating other Christians. However, before I began following people there was one shining moment about which I want to tell you.

On a snowy North Dakota night, I had a difficult choice to make for a girl of fifteen. In the little town where I was born, there was a party at one home and a cottage prayer meeting at another on the same night. I chose the cottage prayer meeting.

The little brown frame house was packed with people. I looked around, as teenagers do, and couldn't spot a single person my age. My first thought was to get out, but the house was small and too crowded. The thought came to me, hadn't I already made my choice? God knew, didn't He, when I asked Him where to go that Friday night, that there wouldn't be anyone my age at the meeting?

I stayed. There was a Bible reading. Then everyone knelt. So did I. I felt I was only an onlooker. How did they know when to pray? Who told them? My heart beat faster. Should I pray, too? Where, I asked myself, did *that* idea come from? Me pray aloud? In front of all those people? When I was the only teenager present? Probably no one even knew I was there.

Faster and faster went my heart. The person who had been praying for some time stopped. There was silence. No. No. No! I couldn't break it! Let someone else do it. Cautiously I asked myself, who am I arguing with about this thing? Myself? Could it be that God was asking me to pray aloud in front of all these people? What difference could it make to God if I did or if I didn't?

While I was struggling with my thoughts and my objections, an older lady began to pray. I sighed with temporary relief.

Why, I said to myself, she can't even speak English! No one can understand a word she is saying, and here she is praying where people can hear her. I listened. A sentence or two in German, a smattering of English, then more German.

I withheld further judgment and listened again. Suddenly I felt my heart was being held in God's hand. The old German lady was crying! And she wasn't ashamed to be praying or crying. The tenderness in her voice told me that her tears were not those of frustration, but of real love for her Lord. She was speaking *to Him. Not to us.* And He was there. I knew it. *He was there.*

The rapid conversation in my heart went on: *You* can speak English. *You* belong to God in a new way since last June and are *you* still afraid? That was enough. I recognized the voice of Jesus. I would pray aloud, and I would speak straight to Him. I would not be afraid and I would not care if there were tears, and I would not care if my words got tangled up and I would not care if my prayer was like the others or if it wasn't. I would forget the people and just think about Him.

And I did. "Dear Lord Jesus . . . " I heard myself praying aloud for the first time in my life. And I did cry and my words did get tangled, but it was all right. I had spoken to Him. He was there.

He had been there all the time I was arguing with myself. And He was there when I spoke to Him aloud with other people listening.

As the snow crunched under my feet that cold winter night on my way home, my heart was warm with the freshness of talking with Jesus Christ. I had met Him. I had had my first flash of insight about prayer.

Perhaps I understood as only the very young understand easily, that He meant it when He said,

> . . . where two or three
> are gathered together in my
> name, there am I
> in the midst of them.

The second one

After that first "shining moment" when I knew that prayer was talking person to person with the Lord Jesus, I was no longer afraid to pray aloud. He loved me and I loved Him, and all the world was new, and I was young and life was good. I wanted to be the best kind of Christian there was. I wanted to learn how to pray in the right way, and began to keep my ears open to see how other people prayed and what they said and how they said it.

Since I was no longer afraid to pray in public, it was easy to pick up pointers and to begin to use them. Several things impressed me immediately. The language people used, and the way they addressed God. I also noticed that when the pastor's wife prayed, people said "Amen" and "Yes, Lord." When she said the correct thing they seemed to be encouraged and agreed with her and said so. It bothered me for a while, but soon I found myself praying like Mrs. O. and wanting to say things that would make people say "Amen" to my prayers, also.

Apparently, the tone of voice was something to watch, if one wanted to get anywhere in prayer. An unconsciously dramatic tone which was different and pitched higher than the usual conversation voice seemed preferable. This tone kept climbing and climbing until it reached a climax, and then came down and started again. It sounded like a good way to persuade God that one meant business.

God knows I was in dead earnest over the whole matter. I think I became rather restless sometimes, but wouldn't have admitted it to anyone for the world. The first inkling I had of this restlessness was when I heard one of the ladies in the church pray. She climbed the heights and prayed around the world. Suddenly I "heard" the tone of her voice, and thought to myself, if I didn't know who is praying, I wouldn't know it was Mrs. R. I wonder if God wants us to talk to Him in that unnatural tone of voice? How can we be our real selves if we pray like that?

I was shocked at myself for thinking such thoughts. But the idea wouldn't go away.

"How can God talk to you when you are praying, if you are shouting at Him like that? Why don't you give Him a chance to say a word?" I was a bit uneasy, I'll admit, trying to answer that one. But I put it carefully aside, because who was I to try to reform the prayer meeting? Besides, "being spiritual" was pretty important to me, because I was just at the age when being approved meant everything.

It was a glorious day when I was "approved" by a foreign missionary society and sent to China at the age of twenty as a secretary in the missionary office. I was deeply sincere in that I felt this was where God was guiding me, and I tried with my whole heart to enter into all that pertained to the mission work.

On the field there was the regular Friday night staff prayer meeting. The entire evening was devoted to the meeting. We sang, had a message from the Bible, a time of talking over problems concerning the work among the Chinese, and then we prayed. Everyone prayed, and the prayers were long and detailed and no one missed that meeting unless he were ill.

As I look back upon it now, I remember the devotion and sincerity of my own heart, and I still deeply love the friends I made.

We were all together on our knees in the same room, each with love for the other, and each with a common purpose. However, I began to realize we were each making a little speech to the Lord when our turn came. I know we were supposed to pray silently with the one who was praying out loud, but when we all covered the same ground — well, I found that I was trying to think how I could start my prayer with more "colorful" words. How I could put more "action" into my prayer, how I could make it sound more "spiritual," and how I could take hold of the promises with more faith than the others. I wanted to word it differently from the persons who had prayed before me and make it sound more important and interesting.

God forgive me for the pride that wanted my prayer to be different! God forgive me for the times I deliberately planned my opening paragraph just to make it sound better than the others!

And God forgive me for the times I chose a chair near the bookcases, so that (kneeling in prayer) when things became dull, I could quietly glance through the shelves and make a mental note, and often a penciled note, of the books I wanted to read.

And God forgive me for those times when I actually pulled out a book, and using my jacket around my shoulders as a shield, leafed through it during the prayer meeting.

God forgive me, too, for the times I just plain fell asleep on my knees during those long sessions of prayer. After my turn was over, it wasn't too hard to do.

The years of service on the field piled up. The prayer meetings piled up. My rebellions piled up. And yet knowing the sincerity and the depth of the spiritual lives of those with whom I worked and prayed, I couldn't bring myself to admit my rebellion. Neither could I really face the lack of depth in my own prayer life.

I felt I was doing the best I knew. Wasn't that all the Lord expected of me?

The third one

Through a near fatal illness and other rough experiences, God began to take care of my rebellions through His great love. He began to teach me to listen to His voice.

The third prayer meeting, which was so simple and yet to be so

17

revolutionary, took place a few months after my time as a mission office secretary ended. I was living in Peiping, China, studying the language and trying to identify myself with the Chinese people in every possible way.

Very soon, a group of high school and college students were asking for instruction in English, and they were interested in reading the English New Testament. Needing help, I called on my long-time friend Mildred Rice, who was living on the same mission compound. We divided the group and met regularly with them.

The young people brought their problems to us, and quite naturally Mildred and I began taking them to the Lord in prayer together.

One never-to-be-forgotten afternoon, we knelt in my little Chinese apartment to pray for several of these students by name, and for the class that evening.

As I remember, Mildred was praying for Yu-fu in a situation that concerned her sister-in-law. Now I'd forgotten to tell Mildred that Yu-fu had sent a little note to me that morning and that the situation for which Mildred was praying had already been cleared up. Her prayer was already answered and she didn't know it!

Without thinking, I interrupted her prayer, and continued it as mine, "We thank Thee, Lord, that Thou hast already answered our prayer. Yu-fu has already been able to forgive her sister-in-law."

I stopped, startled by my own daring at interrupting Mildred's prayer. There was a moment of silence, then with great relief both of us sat back and laughed.

"Why, isn't that something!" said Mildred, meaning both the early answer to her prayer, *and* the natural way in which the news about Yu-fu had popped out.

We settled down to pray again, but with a sense of joy, of lightness, of the Lord's presence very near.

I prayed, "Lord, art Thou trying to teach us something through this incident? Should we give Thee more opportunity as we are praying to get Thy ideas through to us? Would that give the Holy Spirit more opportunity to guide us as we pray?"

18

Then with the freedom which comes with a new discovery, I stopped praying and spoke to Mildred.

"Do you know what? I believe the Lord taught us something just now! Instead of each of us making a prayer-speech to Him, let's talk things over with Him, including Him in it, as we do when we have a conversation."

She took it right up, "Yes, and we could bring up one person or one situation at a time, and both of us pray back and forth about it, until we feel we have touched God, until our hearts are at rest."

I agreed with her thoroughly. But by then I was excitedly remembering something else and had my Bible, hunting a passage in Matthew. There it was.

Again I say unto you, That if two of you shall agree on earth as touching any thing that they shall ask, it shall be done for them of my Father which is in heaven.

For where two or three are gathered together in my name, there am I in the midst of them.
Matthew 18:19, 20

We were definitely on holy ground and we knew it. In a few moments of silence, we turned our attention to the Lord Jesus, who being alive and with us and in us had just told us again,

Where two . . . are gathered
in my name,
there am I
in the midst of them.

And we understood Him in a new way.

Quietly, reverently and with a sharp awareness that Another was with us, we began to *converse with Him* about our friends. All the "padding" of unnecessary prayer-language slipped away. We spoke face to face, knowing that He cared for the ones we brought to Him. There seemed to be no need of the final Amen at the close of each prayer. We were talking with Him and with each other. I spoke, and she spoke, and we waited for Him to reply in that still, small voice within our hearts.

We were in His presence.

We were talking to and with Him.

As we knelt there that afternoon, I experienced a memory flash-back. I remembered that first "shining moment" when I spoke to Jesus Christ at the little cottage prayer meeting in North Dakota. After all these years, He was giving my "shining moment" back to me, but with a new reality because I was older.

I worshiped Him in silent wonder, knowing that from now on there would be no more dullness, no more self-conscious conformity, no more imitation.

This was not a new technique we had discovered. It was too natural and too familiar to be new. Perhaps it was merely an unexpected turning back to the kind of child-like communion with Him which God intended in the first place.

We didn't think this far that day. We were just overjoyed.

CHAPTER 2

Prayer Is a Dialogue

The discovery that Mildred Rice and I made that afternoon in Peiping, China, began to reach deep into our hearts. It was as though a shade had been raised and a new day flooded our prayer lives. I don't know why we didn't go out and tell everyone what had happened. There was still a holy quietness about having met the Lord person to person. Perhaps we were afraid that those older than we might by some chance remark pull the shade down.

A new understanding had come, and although we didn't know it then, we were going to make more and more discoveries. Discoveries which would heal the rebellious places in both of us. New insights which would remove much of the traditionalism which cluttered our prayer habits. The new thing was: we had become conscious of His presence with us.

Praying in a conversational tone, one of the first things we noticed was that unconsciously we were dropping some of the familiar prayer language. Especially the old Quaker forms, the beautiful old Quaker forms of thee, thou, and thy, together with the King James English, with its didst, dost, wouldst, hadst, walketh, sinneth and so on.

We were speaking to the Lord with the simplicity of a child talking to his father in his own language. Was it right? Or was it wrong?

We began to investigate. I was an English major in college, and remembered that when the King James Bible was translated, back in the time of Shakespeare, there were two general types of English spoken. A high and a low English. The high English (you, me, yours) was used for the royal family, nobility and for special ceremonies. The low English (thou, thee, thy) was used in the home, intimately with the family, and in addressing God.

As time went on this usage was reversed. The forms used for royalty became everyday family terms and today we all say you, me, yours. However, the old terms persisted with the Quakers at all times, and with the religious people at church and at prayer. The King James Bible was translated into English during the Shakespearean period, and so the low form, the familiar endearing family terms were used: thy, thou, thee. And they have come down to us today in our English Bible and in our religious services. The original languages from which our English Bible came to us make no such distinction.

I realize that many sincerely feel they are showing disrespect in God's presence if they address Him in any form but "Thou." A little of the language background and history will set their minds at rest, and help them relax and be in a more natural attitude for prayer, which is simply conversing with God.

I, for one, love the poetry of the old terms, and always shall. I especially love to hear them used in a Sunday morning worship service. I understand perfectly that you may love them, too, and would rather not make any change. And you can be assured that God understands this also. After all, it isn't the words we say nor how we say them, it is the open heart attitude which God seeks. I don't believe it makes any difference to Him. He simply longs for us to speak person to person with Him.

If you are beginning to feel that there is a dullness when you pray, or a curtain through which you do not seem able to penetrate, why not deliberately and thoughtfully use everyday English in addressing God? A change, however temporary, usually brings freshness. He is there. He is there with you. He may slip your mind, but you never slip His mind. The different use of a pronoun may be the means through which a new awareness of His presence will come to you.

Prayer is the expression of the human heart in conversation with God. The more natural the prayer, the more real He becomes. It has all been simplified for me to this extent: prayer is a dialogue between two persons who love each other.

CHAPTER 3

What Is Conversational Prayer?

The term "conversational prayer" is not an unusual one. Neither is it original. I've found many groups of young people and adults using this direct, honest approach to God. Yet the word conversation needs to be clearly understood.

What is conversation?

It is a method which should provide communication between two or more people. Unfortunately, it is usually listed among the lost arts of today.

To understand conversational prayer, it will be a great help if we get the following four points about real conversation clearly in our minds.

1. When we converse, we *become aware.* Aware of the other person, his rights, his privileges, his feeling, and if we converse long enough, his total personality.

2. Good conversation implies that we must take turn about and do it gracefully. When one person does all the talking we call it (if we are polite) a monologue.

3. Finally, it should be clear that to converse we *must stick to the same subject,* and pursue it by turns. We are, in a sense, the

listening and speaking members of a team. We have agreed to agree upon our subject of conversation, and to do this each one must decide what is relevant and important at the moment.

4. To carry on a conversation of any significance or interest, each person must use his memory to recall, his patience to wait, his alertness to jump in, his willingness to get out, and above all his capacity to stay on the subject. In other words, *he should be in tune.*

How does all this apply to prayer?

Let me tell you a true story.

Several years ago while I was visiting San Diego State College in California, Ray Williamson, president of the Christian student group, invited me to attend their daily prayer meeting. He pointed to a large tree on the far campus and said, "We meet in a circle around that big tree for fifteen minutes each noon. Meet me here at twelve-thirty sharp and I'll go over with you."

Later, as we walked across the campus toward the big tree, the following conversation took place.

"Is there any special method you follow in your prayer meetings?" I asked.

"Yes, there is," replied Ray. "I usually start, and then the person next to me prays, and we go on around the circle until everyone has prayed."

Now, I knew that I would very much like to introduce conversational prayer to Ray and his group. But I didn't want to push.

I started with a question. "Ray, how does that give the Holy Spirit opportunity to lead you while you pray?"

He looked at me as we walked. "What do you mean?"

I tried to explain. "Well, you see, it's like this. The Holy Spirit within us moves on our hearts and starts our concerns and our love, as well as our requests. Could it be possible that in simply going around a circle, humanly speaking, you might 'quench the Spirit'?"

"Quench the Spirit?"

"Yes, by following a set pattern. That makes it difficult for the

Spirit to move us as we pray, and to make us aware of what He is saying as we pray. Didn't you ever have a wonderful prayer idea right while the other fellow was praying, and say to yourself, 'Now I must be sure to remember *that* and pray about it when my turn comes,' and then when your turn came you couldn't for the life of you remember what it was?"

Ray laughed. "I'm beginning to see what you're driving at, Ros, and it makes sense. Why don't you tell all of us about it, and show us how? Right now."

"Right now?" I looked to see if he really meant it.

We had already been standing by the big tree for several moments, and the group was gathering.

"Yes, right now," he repeated, and stepping into the circle, called the group together. "Ros has a few keen ideas for us, and I know they will help us have a better prayer meeting."

I spoke to them briefly, knowing the fifteen minutes would go by quickly.

"Instead of going around the circle today, let's remember consciously that *the Lord Jesus is right here,* in the center of this circle with us. He promised, 'where two or three are gathered, there am I.' Let's *speak directly to Him,* simply, honestly, just as we talk to anyone in whom we have real confidence. Let's say 'I' when we mean I, and 'we' if we mean the whole group.

"Another important thing is to *pray by subjects.* If someone starts to pray for Joe Blow, two or three of the rest of you feel perfectly free to pray for him, also. Be direct and simple. Then let's wait a moment before introducing a new name. The Spirit will guide you. You can each pray four or five times if you want to, but let's keep to one subject at a time, and pray back and forth. As we open our hearts, the Holy Spirit will guide us concerning who to pray for, what to pray for and when to pray."

Teenagers are quick to grasp new ideas. They were right with me, all of them. I made a quick review.

"Now remember, the Lord is here. We are speaking to Him. Pray in short sentences, and then let someone else have a chance. He will guide us."

There was silence.

I prayed first. "Lord Jesus, thank You that You are here. You said You would be, and all of us want to thank You, and worship You. (Pause) Guide us now, as to whom we should pray for first."

Ray took it up: "Lord, I want to pray for Tony P., that Italian boy in my swim class. He's my buddy, and I've been wanting to talk with him about You, but I haven't done it. Please help me."

A young man across the circle took it next: "Why, Lord, I hadn't any idea Ray was in Tony's swim class. I've already talked to him about You. Bless Ray real good, and give him faith and courage and love for Tony. And help us to work together."

A girl in the circle gasped audibly. "Oh, how wonderful!" Her spontaneous prayer continued, "Lord, I sit right *next to Tony* in an English Lit. Class, and I've already loaned him my *HIS* magazine. I was just wishing Tony knew some real Christian guy who'd talk to him. Why, isn't this wonderful! I had no idea that both Ray and Ted knew Tony!"

Several members of the group prayed for these three and their further contacts with Tony, and for Tony that his heart might be open to receive Christ as his Saviour.

I prayed, "Lord, guide Ray and Ted very definitely. Show them the next step. Show them what You want them to do tomorrow. Help them show Your kind of love to Tony in some definite way."

Ray couldn't wait any longer. He spoke up, and to the whole group. "Say, isn't this great! Hey, this is really neat!" And looking at his wrist watch, "We've got about five minutes more to pray."

Those last five minutes were just as wonderful as the first ten. When the group broke up to go to classes, several of them including Ray walked back with me.

"Ros, tell us more. Why, we were really living just then. This makes prayer alive. What else can you tell us? Is there any more? Shall we just keep on like this?"

"There is just one thing that comes to my mind right now," I replied, not wanting to load them down with too many details which would in any way disturb the joy of their new discovery.

Turning to Ray, I said, "You know what you told me before the meeting about praying around the circle?"

"Yes?"

"Well, when you pray that way you just naturally assume that each person who attends wants to pray, and is willing to pray. Right?"

"Yes," said Ray, slowly thinking it over. "Oh, I think I see what you are driving at, Ros. You mean that there might be someone present who just wants to listen, and *not* pray. Hey, do you suppose anyone who's *not* a Christian might want to come to a prayer meeting?" he finished in surprise.

"That's what I've found," I said, "especially persons with whom I have already talked, and whose hearts are wide open to know the truth. I've known people like that to come, and sometimes the very first time they pray aloud in spite of themselves. The Lord is so near and so real when a group is talking conversationally with Him. And I've seen non-believers walk right into life with Christ just by speaking to Him personally."

Ray was really excited.

"That makes wonderful sense, Ros. After all, when we talk to Christ we're speaking right to Truth, Himself. He said, 'I am the Truth.' If a person really wants to know the Truth, what better way is there than to get into a group where it's easier to begin to talk right to God."

That student had struck a deep note.

When we pray, *to whom* are we really speaking?

See page 87, for the helpful outline, *Conversational Prayer.*

See page 88, *Meditation,* for teaching the subject: God loves you. This is the basis of all true prayer.

CHAPTER 4

To Whom Should We Pray?

To whom should we pray?

Does it make any difference whether we pray to the Father or to the Son, or to the Holy Spirit?

This question is asked over and over. If it does make a difference, we should find out, for God has good reasons for everything that concerns us. If it doesn't make a difference, we should also find out. The fine sensitive relationship which exists between God's Spirit and our spirit needs all the relaxed quietness and receptivity possible. Uninformed ignorance, sluggish unconcern or dull conformity are all number one enemies which need to be chased out of our lives.

Is your prayer life alive? Are your prayer times too few and too far between? Have you been bogging down and slowing up? And are you looking back with regret and longing at earlier years when prayer had more meaning to you? I confess this happens periodically with me.

Occasionally, we should face our need for fresh beginnings. If you have been praying to the Father, and have never addressed the Son in prayer, why not get on speaking terms with Him, too?

If you have never addressed the Holy Spirit in prayer, you have a great Counselor who is waiting to get acquainted with you. He knows all about you.

Does it make any difference to whom you pray?

Whose presence are you aware of when you pray? Is your heart at all affected by the name or names by which you address God when you pray? Or are you more concerned about the content of your prayer? Or perhaps your concern may be just to get it over with, so you can relax again.

May I tell you about a college girl who had been completely unaware of the name she was using when she prayed? And of the amazing difference it made in her relationship to God when she did become aware?

Marian was a college sophomore when I first met her. She was one of a small group of girls who met to plan and pray with me about how best to present Jesus Christ to their friends on campus. Each noon we met for a short time of prayer. We were learning to pray conversationally. After I'd heard her pray once, I was concerned. After the second time, I prayed, "Lord if You want me to speak with Marian and give her a few pointers, put it into her heart to come and see me." (I believe in definite, time-limit, faith-sized requests for some things, and will develop this subject in a later chapter.)

That very night there was a knock at my door. It was Marian. I was glad to see her and said so. I even told her that I'd asked the Lord to send her.

"You did?" she asked. "Why?"

"Because I see a great God-potential in you and I think a little talk might help you. You won't mind, will you, if I talk with you about something I've noticed?"

She told me to go right ahead.

"Marian, whom do you pray to?"

She hesitated a moment, "I guess I pray to the Lord Jesus."

"Do you?" I waited a moment to let her think. "What do you call Him?"

"Uh — uh — Dear Lord Jesus," she said uncertainly.

"Well, tell me, Marian, do you do this both in your own private prayers and when you pray with others?"

"Why, uh — yes, I think I do," Marian looked a little puzzled. "Ros, why are you asking me this? Tell me."

So I told her. I had taken the liberty of timing her prayer the second time I'd heard her. And I had a reason. The prayer lasted one minute, and in that time she had used the name "God" thirty-three times! She had used His Name as a punctuation mark, and not as though she were speaking to a real, living Person.

I gave her an example of the way she prayed, so she would understand: "O God, we thank You, God, that we can come into Your Presence, God. God, we need You today, God. God, will You help us, O God, to live for You today, God."

She was embarrassed and surprised. Fortunately, she had an open mind. We had a comfortable talk on the subject, and then she asked, "Could we pray again now?" We did, and this time, by her own choice, she started, "Dear Lord Jesus . . . " instead of her habitual, "Dear God . . . . " She prayed slowly, thoughtfully, with many pauses, and used His Name meaningfully. She *was* speaking to Someone, *He* was there!

Suddenly, with tears, she looked up. "Oh, Ros, I feel as if I've become a Christian all over again! I was not aware of what I was doing, I guess I was praying to be praying, if there is such a thing. I didn't really know to whom I was praying. Now I know. It's Jesus Christ!"

In my own efforts to learn the true meaning of prayer, and to recognize His presence, I personally have found it more helpful to address most of my prayers to the Lord Jesus. And yet there are times when I find myself praying to the Father, or to the Holy Spirit. I searched the New Testament with this one thought in mind: to find when and why each member of the Trinity was addressed. I had a page in my notebook for each, and from this study I gained confidence and knowledge.

I am not trying to give you a pat theological answer. I am only trying to give you the simple answers I found for myself in regard to whom I may address my prayer. But out of this study I have

31

also found a simplicity concerning the whole Christian faith. I discovered that when this mystifying subject of the Trinity is brought up and talked about and explained (inasmuch as we are able), it begins of its own accord to form the basis of our belief in the Person of Jesus Christ.

There is one God. Not three. He is three Persons but one in essence and substance. The dictionary definition of essence is this: That *in being* which underlies all outward manifestations and is permanent and unchangeable. In other words, the very substance of.

Why has God shown Himself to us in three Persons? Where did this idea originate?

Jesus Christ Himself taught us (mainly in the Gospel of John) that He and the Father are one. *Jesus Christ is the Father defined.* No one called God "Father" before Jesus came. The complete fifth chapter of John is a discourse on the equality of the Father and the Son. No one knew what God was really like until Jesus of Nazareth came to visit this earth and show who God really is.

Where does the Holy Spirit come into the picture? Jesus said (and I paraphrase from John 14:16-20): I am going away to My Father, but I will send the Comforter, the Spirit of truth to be with you forever. I will not leave you helpless orphans, I will come to you. In that day you will know that I am in My Father, and you in Me, and I in you.

Paul tells us in II Corinthians 3:17 that the Holy Spirit is the Spirit of the Lord Jesus in us.

If you seem to be having difficulty in understanding that three persons can be of one essence, here is an illustration which has helped me. The compound H_2O is found in three forms, gas, liquid and solid (air, water, ice) but they are all composed of the same basic elements — two atoms of hydrogen and one of oxygen. Each has a significance and use of its own, but all are composed of exactly the same elements. There is no contradiction among them, just as there is no contradiction in the members of the Godhead.

From an old Scotch Presbyterian book I copied a diagram of the Trinity which I have found most helpful.

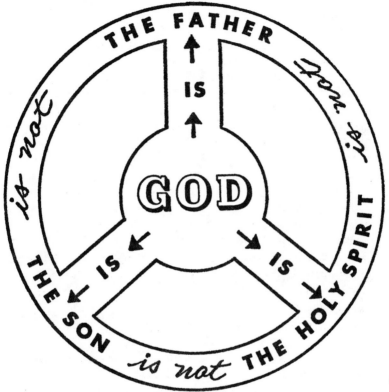

A Diagram of the Trinity

Notice that the name GOD is all-inclusive and when you start from the center of the circle, the fact that they are all one becomes evident: God is the Father, God is the Son, God is the Spirit. But go around the outer edge of the circle, and you find the Father is not the Son, the Son is not the Spirit, the Spirit is not the Father. Their one essence is shown at the center, and their three personalities are shown at the circumference.

Why has God shown Himself to us in three Persons?

God is the great Eternal Being, but we are so limited in all our spiritual concepts that He has given us three different glimpses of Himself, through three different Personalities, but the three are One.

I believe that God must have anticipated this human confusion of ours about Himself. This is surely one of the reasons He visited this earth in the Person of Jesus Christ. As we study Christ's life, death and resurrection, we find ourselves being overcome by the certain knowledge of God's true character.

It is important for us to be able to think of our God as a Person, not an idea, or a principle or even a spiritual concept. It must follow that whatever name we use for Him, that name must have some real meaning for us. There are literally hundreds of names for God in both the Old and New Testament.

How many names do you have for the person most beloved on earth? Does one mean any more than another? The reason is usually a significant one.

We neither offend Him nor pacify Him by the name we choose to use when we speak to Him. His love is unchanging. It is not at all dependent on us or the phrases we use.

Jesus taught us to "Pray to your Father who is in secret." When He was on earth, He prayed to His Father. He taught us to say, "Our Father, which art in heaven." Most of the time He was concealing His own personal glory and identity, both of which have now been revealed. During His earthly days He voluntarily became dependent upon His Father, though from eternity they have been equal.

Jesus invited us to pray in His Name. He assured us that He alone has power to give us eternal life. He taught that all the Father is and has are His. "The Father judgeth no man, but hath committed all judgment unto the Son: That all men should honour the Son, even as they honour the Father. He that honoureth not the Son honoureth not the Father which hath sent him" (John 5:22, 23; 14:13).

Jesus Christ was worshiped by those who knew who He was, both during His earthly life and after His resurrection. One of the central themes of the Book of Revelation is that the Lamb will be the object of our worship through all eternity.

For an Old Testament look at the names of the coming God-Man, there is Isaiah 9:6: "For unto us a child is born, unto us a son is given: and the government shall be upon his shoulder: and his name shall be called Wonderful, Counsellor, The mighty God, The everlasting Father, The Prince of Peace."

Paul tells us that every knee in heaven and on earth and under the earth will bow at the Name of Jesus.

Is Jesus Christ God? Your answer to this question will determine your attitude toward Him. Is the deity of the Son of God actual? Is this Scriptural? A positive answer to these questions has meant the beginning of a personal relationship with Jesus Christ to many searching people.

Before I came to know Stella Newbill of Seattle (she is now my good friend) she had been seeking God for some time. It was easy to come to the point. "Stella, I hear you have been reading Unity. Are you receiving any help?"

"Who told you, Ros? I'd be interested to know," said Stella.

So I told her and she smiled. "Yes, I have been reading Unity, because I need to have some prayers answered. But I still have one big question. Is Jesus Christ God?"

From there we began a conversation neither of us will ever forget. An hour or so later, we knelt together in prayer. Stella quietly in her own words, and for the first time in her life, acknowledged Jesus Christ as her Lord and her God. A personal relationship began for her that day because, knowing who God really is, she could put her trust in Him.

For the past few years she has been an amazingly creative and effective witness to Jesus Christ in her community. One of the first persons to be reached for Christ through Stella was her husband, Art. Now both of them are strong and peaceful in spite of a physical illness which I have seen defeat persons who have been Christians for most of their lives. They

35

are both sure of God's ultimate intentions toward them because they know what Jesus Christ is like, and they know that He and the Father are one.

Our God is infinite, but we are so earthbound that He has done everything possible to help us grasp and understand something of His eternal dimensions. He has given us three views of Himself, and yet there is more. Like the vast ocean stretching away, there is so much more.

I am forever convinced that anyone who comes to the place of realizing that God and Jesus Christ are one and the same, has reached a new understanding of what prayer really is. Somehow it is easy to speak to Jesus Christ. After all, we know that He knows what it feels like to be us.

> *Wherefore in all things it behoved him to be made like unto his brethren . . . (Hebrews 2:17).*

CHAPTER 5

Prayer Begins a New Relationship

In this chapter I would like to tell you how conversational prayer, or conversing with God, has provided a simple way by which people have come into the Kingdom of God. The simplicity of responding person to person to Jesus Christ seems to break down all barriers. Yet it is not prayer that is emphasized, nor is prayer the important thing. Christ is the center, and prayer is the means by which we begin to respond to Him. In a moment I'll share with you two stories which illustrate what I mean.

First let us think back about the things we have already learned about conversing with God.

We know to whom we are speaking. We are not talking with an unknown God, but to the God-Man, Jesus Christ, who was in all points tempted like as we are, so that we can feel freer to come to Him with our temptations. We have come to a clearer knowledge of the greatness of our God, who has shown Himself to us as the great Three in One.

We have also discussed some of the things that keep us from intimate conversation with Him: The lack of knowledge of who Jesus Christ is, failure to remember He is constantly present with us; the language barriers, the tradition-bound prayer habits, self-consciousness or desire for the approval of others.

In order to overcome these barriers we need not only to read, but also to begin to put what we have read into daily prayer practice. We need to learn the art of conversation. We need to learn to pray in His Presence, and to let Him speak with us, to be in tune with Him until we are willing to hear what He has to say to us.

There is an intimate relationship between the Shepherd and the sheep which is always initiated by the Shepherd Himself. But there is something for the sheep to do when he enters the fold. He has to be willing to hear and respond to the Shepherd's voice. Frequently we need the help of one or two other "sheep" who already know His voice in order to make our response a complete one. *We need to learn to pray with one another.* We are all sheep of His pasture, and we need to be together.

However, more is involved than merely being willing to pray together. How does one *know* when he is in the fold? *When* does one receive eternal life? The answer is simple. When he comes to Jesus. When he feels that *need* which the Spirit has put into his heart, and when he begins to respond to Jesus Christ, as the God who can forgive his sins and make him a member of His fold.

This brings us to those wonderful words which the Lord gave us in John 10:27. When *do* we become His sheep?

I remember Grace, a brilliant Chinese university student, who was about to complete her study for her doctorate in chemistry. Her chief concern for weeks had been the fact that she wanted to be a Christian and was not. One day we sat together at a study table talking about what Jesus Christ had already done on the Cross, and I promised her that because He is alive, speaking directly to Him would bring her the assurance she needed. Still she hesitated.

We turned to John's Gospel and read chapter 10 verse 27 together: "My sheep hear my voice and I know them, and they follow me; And I give them eternal life . . . ." I asked her to notice the sequence of the verbs. My sheep *hear* my voice. They *follow* me. I *give* them eternal life. Then I asked, when did they become His sheep, before or after Jesus gave them eternal life? We looked again. The first step is to hear His voice and begin to follow the Shepherd, and then He does all the giving.

She admitted she had heard His voice. But when did this "sheep" belong to Jesus? There it was, right in the beginning of the verse, *My* sheep. Because He already considered her His, she was able to hear His voice! Suddenly she saw it from His viewpoint. This is a mystery I cannot explain, but in His great eternal knowledge, He knows when to call us. There is no past, present or future with the Lord. It is all an eternal *now* with Him.

There was silence at the table where we sat. We bowed our heads, and I said, "Thank You Lord, for showing Grace Your viewpoint." And she prayed, "Lord Jesus, I want to thank You. This is my first time to speak to You. So You've been here all along!" Then I thanked Him again. And quite naturally, Grace prayed again and thanked Him for forgiving her sins and for giving her eternal life.

For a moment neither of us spoke. Then she began to pray for her family and for her friends. The barrier was down. Speaking directly to Him had made Him a real Person. Knowing, finally, that Jesus Christ had loved her from the beginning, there was only one thing left to do, and that was to respond by speaking to Him.

Last Year in New York City I was having lunch in the Manhattan Hotel Coffee Shop with a professional woman who had come to know her need of Jesus Christ through adverse circumstances. She tells the story in her own words in a letter she wrote to her mother; a copy of which she sent me:

"Christ was always a waiting figure to me, who charmed and glowed, but it seemed He was always 'outside me,' always slipping away from me. It seemed to me He was a waiting potential, nothing more: And I was sure it was His fault. Ros said, 'But Marj, have you *asked* Him to come in, have you said, "Welcome, abide with me" to Him? No, I just hadn't, Mother. Never, not once: He scared me rather. For no reason at all. Ros said, 'Do you want to, now?' I said yes, help me. It appeared that we were having a casual coffee shop conversation. Ros prayed. And then I said, 'Lord Jesus, I love You, too.' I meant it fully, with all my heart. That is why the past two months or so have been so different as to be beyond belief. There is a sheer, keen joy of living which I never experienced before. I don't know much yet, and may make mistakes, but I know Jesus Christ will take care of me."

I have included the experiences of these two women in this chapter since I have observed that a pious prayer in an emotionally charged atmosphere can turn some people the other direction, while an open, natural conversation with the Lord Himself, who is always right there with us, can make a hard step easier. It is not easy to turn the controls of your life over to Another when you can't see Him. But when you know He's there and speak with Him and to Him naturally, the barriers go down.

The response of your heart to His initial love for you releases your love for Him.

You discover that He has long sought you, called to you, prepared for you, loved you. And now you know the way into the fold: Response to the Shepherd Himself, Jesus Christ.

Have you responded to Him?

Have you spoken to Him, simply, naturally, out of the need of your heart? In your own words?

He is there.

If you are interested in knowing Him, or in knowing His will for your life, you can come. Your very interest proves that you have heard His voice. And He has said:

Everyone who has heard . . . comes to me.

Further Bible reading on the subject of this chapter: Matthew 11:25-30; John 6:35-51; John 10.

See *Meditation* on page 88. This is an assurance of God's love for you.

CHAPTER 6

Why Pray Aloud Together?

Why should I pray aloud with someone else? Jesus Himself said "Enter into thy closet, and pray to thy Father which is in secret."

Yes, Jesus said this. Then, "Why should I pray aloud with someone else?" could very well be the question you are asking. I am aware that so far we have seemed to emphasize group prayer, but what has been said may apply to our personal devotions as well. There are many reasons for this emphasis on praying together which I shall continue to share; but I do understand your question about the necessity of praying with others.

Jesus taught us to go into our closets and pray to our Father in secret. Have you read the verses that go with this one? You will find them in Matthew 6:1-14. Jesus is counseling us against praying for the approval of others, and telling us that there is only One to whom we should pray.

Since you object to praying with others because of the words of Jesus "Enter into your closet" do you then deeply desire to keep His words? And do you often enter into your closet and pray in secret? And do you find new life and new love through meeting Him there? These are pointed questions, but unless we are honest with ourselves, we can go on and on, missing the wonder the Lord has for us.

Practically every real revelation of Himself and His will has come to me *after* He has broken down the barriers which have been erected. Erected in simple self-defense or fear. Erected because of environment or background. It is quite possible that these barriers are among the "mountains" about which the Lord Jesus speaks in Mark 11:23. "Whoever says to this mountain, 'Be taken up and thrown into the sea!' and entertains no inner doubt, but believes that what he says will happen, it shall be so for him" (Berkeley).

We shall talk more about removing "mountains" in the chapter on faith-sized requests. However, we can look at some of them right here, honestly and openly, and we can begin to see them disintegrate and slip away into the "sea." The mountain of fear exists mainly behind closed doors of aloneness. Open the door, share with others, and the chances are you will look in vain for your "mountain."

Jesus did teach us to go into our closets and pray to our Father in secret, because He knows that when we shut out everyone else and concentrate on being with Him, on being conscious of Him, our heart-wounds are healed and we are made whole. There, alone in the quietness, He can speak to us and comfort us and guide us and pour His fresh life and love into us. Praying is like eating; you must eat for yourself, no one else can do it for you.

But Jesus Christ also taught us to pray together and to say, "Our Father which art in heaven." This is the only entire prayer He gave us. Yet He made many references to prayer.

He said: "Keep on asking and it will be given you." Whatever you ask for in prayer, believe — trust and be confident — that it will be granted to you, and you will [get it]." "— I Myself will grant — whatever you may ask in My name." "Ask and keep on asking and you will receive, so that your joy (gladness, delight) may be full and complete" (Matthew 7:7; Mark 11:24; John 14:13; 16:24, Amplified).

42

More than any other teaching Jesus gave us on prayer, I think I love the one Matthew recorded in chapter 18, verses 19 and 20, and the surrounding verses. Before writing this chapter I read them again from seven different versions and translations: King James, Revised Standard, Amplified New Testament, Berkeley, Lamsa, Phillips and Williams. They all throw new light on Matthew 18:19,20 but I want to quote from the direct, simple Williams' translation: "Again, I tell you, if only two of you on earth agree on what they pray for, they will get it from my Father in heaven. For wherever two or three have met as my disciples, I am right there with them."

Why pray together? Because Jesus promised that when two of His disciples (that means us today) meet to pray, He will be there with them. Our risen, living Lord said and meant what He said: "I am there, right among them" (Phillips). "There am I in the midst of them" (King James). In a particular way, in a particular promise, *He is present.* I have experienced it again and again, and so can you.

Why pray together?

Because Jesus knows that the problems of life press in upon us when we are alone until the spirit is almost broken; the mind refuses to accept reality and so escapes into a world of its own. Burdens shared become lighter. "Bear one another's burdens," said Paul. Before I learned the secret of prayer together, I thought that my burdens were greater than anyone else's burdens. Now I know they aren't and now I know a way to help instead of always wanting to be helped.

Why pray together?

Because as we pray the Spirit of our Lord has our attention. He is always conscious of us, but we need to focus our attention and our consciousness upon Him. Then He can whisper to us the plans He has for us. Sometimes these directions come to two or more persons in the group at the same time. We find ourselves in total agreement in all that we are asking. This leaves no room for wavering, for double-mindedness or for doubt. We have agreed in His presence, and He Himself has given us that agreement.

Why pray together?

Because His great heart of love longs and yearns to give us all that we need, whether that need is spiritual, mental, emotional, physical or material. I believe He gives us all He can give, without our direct asking; but when we are consciously in His presence He softens our hearts and our minds, and we find ourselves being changed and enabled to receive. When we pray together we become bold and honest and we ask for things we never intended asking for.

Why pray together?

Praying with other people gives us new sisters and new brothers in Christ. The more we pray with other people the more we begin to trust them, and the more honest we will be about our personal needs. Self-consciousness drops away and we can pray about our real problems, not just surface ones. Genuine "togetherness" is a God-given state, and hearts are joined in His presence. We can depend upon that presence because He has said, "I am right there with them."

If all this and more is waiting for us when we pray with one another and with Him, why is it that so few persons today meet to pray together? We spend hours in time-consuming pleasant conversation. We talk for an hour on the telephone. We all know how to talk. And we talk. Why then do we find so many excuses not to talk with the Lord Jesus, and with each other in His presence?

Even though we practice it little, we believe in prayer and we want to know more about prayer. We want to know more about the simplicity of praying. In a survey conducted on "Sermons America Wants to Hear" by *This Week* magazine, the number one choice was: "How Can I Make Prayer More Effective?" The results of this poll are no surprise to me. Everywhere I go I find a growing interest in prayer.

At this writing, I have just returned from a Michigan church where we held pre-Easter meetings. My friend, Eugenia Price, brought the evening message. The pastor wanted an invitation following the message, but was afraid the people wouldn't go along with it.

This plan came to our minds while we were actually praying together: She would announce an "after-service" in which I would give simple instruction on prayer, using material from this book. We felt that only those with real needs would come. The first night I set out ten chairs in the room adjoining the sanctuary. To our amazement, seventy persons crowded into that room! It was the same night after night. Many of them had never prayed aloud and did not particularly want to pray aloud in front of anyone else. But most of the people did pray — simply, honestly and directly from their hearts.

During the week we were there, families which had never prayed together before began to speak to God conversationally in their homes. A regular church prayer meeting has begun again at the request of the people and the minister. Comfort and togetherness were given to lonely hearts. We left with the certainty that things have only just begun to happen in that Michigan church.

I was convinced more than ever that people do want to pray. All that is needed is simple instruction at the personal level and an opportunity to pray. We don't learn how to pray in six easy lessons, we learn to pray by praying.

But, you say, I am not in that Michigan community. There is no group of people in my church or town with whom I can pray. Then begin to "ask" for someone with whom you can pray. Ask and believe that God can and will give you at least one person with whom you may pray aloud.

Maybe you still have an unconscious block about praying aloud, which will not yield. In the first five chapters of this book we have already talked about many of the problems concerning praying aloud. Perhaps it will help you to look at them again. One of them is bound to be yours:

Chapter 1. Self-defense, what others think, wanting the approval of others, wanting to be "spiritual," fear of imperfection in praying, fear of weeping.

Chapter 2. Long wearisome prayers, stilted in language and static in content, uncreative and without life.

Chapter 3. The language barrier, the King James tongue twisters, the far-awayness of God because you may think He cannot appreciate English as it is spoken today.

Chapter 4. The haziness of your concept of the Triune God. It is difficult to pray to a God you do not know. Prayer to the Father may seem stiff and formal because you fail to understand who the Son and the Holy Spirit really are.

Chapter 5. The impossibility of praying (as a friend) to One with whom we have no relationship. Perhaps your need is to invite Him into your heart, to make a definite commitment of yourself to Him, to believe in Him personally, and to believe that He is a Person whom you can trust.

All the above problems are answered in each of the chapters mentioned. At least they are answered in a way that helped me, and opened the way for me to approach God through Jesus Christ.

The real basis for not wanting to pray with someone else (aside from not wanting to answer the call of the Good Shepherd and come under His authority and His care) is usually human pride. Pride is the basis of all self-consciousness, which in turn is one of the products of being a so-called adult. Children pray easily without self-conflict or self-consciousness. Jesus taught us that we must become as little children to enter, and to live within, the Kingdom of Heaven. As adults we become aware of ourselves and our real or imagined abilities, and will go to any lengths to erect defenses to keep from exposing ourselves as we are.

Do you really want to learn to pray with others? Do you recognize what it is that is holding you back? Then you are "on the way" and it is the Good Shepherd Himself who is leading you.

Anyone who belongs to Jesus Christ, confessing Him as Lord and Saviour, can be delivered from fear of praying in public. The first step is to ask Him to deliver you from this fear. Read II Timothy 1:7. "For God hath not given us the spirit of fear; but of power, and of love, and of a sound mind." Let us ask and receive the gifts He has for us, and refuse all else, in the power of His name.

46

Dietrich Bonhoeffer, in his book *Life Together* (Harpers) helped me tremendously. I defeat my purpose for instance, if I pat myself on the back after I pray aloud, and say to myself, "My, you certainly prayed a good prayer that time!"

A prayer life full of self-conceit and pride would rise no higher than the top of my head, and certainly there would be no unconscious outreach in love to my brother or sister in that prayer group. I would be thinking only of making a good impression, and the unconscious result of such an attitude both upon myself and upon others would leave little room for love.

Go ahead and stumble in your prayers, go ahead and cry. Out of your very weakness your brother is made strong. Out of your own weakness you are made strong by Christ. Out of the inadequacy of your prayer, the inability to express yourself, the shame of your tears, and the urgency of your need, you meet the Saviour who understands you. You are comforted and your brother is strengthened. Out of this weakness your brother, hearing and observing that you are in no better state than he, becomes strong. He is encouraged by your so-called failures that he, too, may meet the Lord in his weakness.

If I pray a "spiritual" sounding, well-padded prayer of which I am proud, who is helped by it? Neither I nor my brother.

Wherever two or three are gathered together, said Jesus, *I am right there with them.*

Wherever two or three are gathered with the Lord, there He is, with all His love revealed and exposed. How? In and by and through one another. And where there is love there is healing. Wherever Jesus Christ is present eternal love is present. When my attention is turned toward Him, and my prayer directed to Him, then His love heals my heart, and I am ready to pray, in love, for my brother or my sister.

> For wherever two or three have met as my disciples, I am right there with them (Williams).

CHAPTER 7

Why Pray Alone?

In the last chapter we thought together about some of the results which come when we pray together. In this chapter we want to think about the important place which secret prayer should have in every believer's life.

There are many important things which the Lord wants to give us which (psychologically) result only from group prayer. To refresh our minds, here are a few of the things we found as we looked into the meaning of Matthew 18:19,20.

When we meet to pray with someone else, *the Lord is present* as a third party. Together we learn to talk, to Him and with Him, in openness and simplicity and without self-consciousness. We leave our heavy burdens at His feet by sharing and agreeing together. Our fears and anxious worries melt away. He speaks and together we learn to listen. He gives us guidance and direction and spiritual healing. He makes us ready to receive all He has to give to us. We acquire new brothers and sisters. We belong to a new family and we begin to learn to take spiritual family responsibilities for one another.

One of the most important things we learned was that even

our weaknesses become sources of strength when we are consciously there in His presence, because *need* is the golden door
of opportunity through which our Saviour meets us face to face.

All this and more comes from just being there together. All
this and more comes from being there, consciously in His
presence. All this and more awaits those who will answer His call
to come apart with Him — alone.

"Rise up, my love, my fair one, and come away. For lo, the
winter is past . . . The flowers appear on the earth; the time of
the singing of birds is come, and the voice of the turtle is heard
in our land . . . . Arise, my love, my fair one, and come away.
O my dove, that art in the clefts of the rock, in the secret places
of the stairs, let me see thy countenance, let me hear thy voice"
(Song of Solomon 2:10-14).

The Good Shepherd knows what His sheep need. They need
the pastures of being together with one another, but they also
need the quiet waters of intimate security — security which
comes from being alone with Him in the secret places.

"My sheep hear my voice, and they follow me."

When have you heard His voice and followed Him into His
secret place? When have you found rest in just being with Him?

Being human, we tend to be heavy-handed in one direction or
the other. Depending on our personality traits, some of us tend
either toward always being with people or always being alone.
These preferences carry over directly into our prayer life. It is
just as eccentric to leave all praying until prayer meeting night
as it is to insist that religion is a private matter and do all our
praying alone. Actually it is quite possible to become so ingrown
in our relationships with God that we "escape" to the closet,
labeling it virtue.

Recently such a young woman came for counseling, and I
discovered that due to strained and broken relationships with
loved ones, she had almost entirely withdrawn from people.
She was finding her "comfort" alone in her room, meditating and
reading and praying. But the results of all this were introspec-
tive and unhealthy.

Why Pray Alone?

49

None of us should hide behind the alibi that "this is the way I am." None of us should say that due to our own reservations, we are unable to be at ease in the presence of other believers, or that we are unable to pray with them. By the same token none of us should say that we cannot learn to be alone in a room for an hour or more with God. In time and with willingness anyone can learn to do both. To have one without the other is like having day without night. They complement one another, they help us to become whole persons.

But the Shepherd will not drive you. He will not drive you either to share the joys of praying with others, nor will He drive you to the intimacy of praying alone. He will wait. He will draw you and keep drawing you until you begin to respond. He waits for you to begin to speak to Him, and to respond from love's freedom, not from love's compulsion. When you are ready, you will find that He has been waiting for you, conscious of you all the time.

There are several practical points which may help you to make this practice of secret prayer part of your daily life.

1. Have a definite place to pray alone. Every time you pass that place, whether it is by a chair, or your bedside, an unused room, a little closet, your desk or your car, you will be reminded that both physical and spiritual refreshment await you there.

2. Anticipate meeting One who loves you in a personal intimate way. Before you arrive at this special place, let your mind constantly say, "I am going to meet Him, I am going to be consciously aware of Him." After you are there, say: "Here in this quiet place, He can show me Himself. I am His. I can put aside all else and worship You, my Lord, and my God."

3. Let your prayers be semi-audible. You *are* speaking to a Person, and hearing your own voice will keep your thoughts centered on Him, although sometimes there will be only deep unspoken torrents of love and adoration welling up from within.

4. Use a daily devotional book, and use some kind of study book to give you needed direction in your daily Bible reading.
(Growth Through Reading, p. 123).

Here it might be well to ask yourself, What does worship really mean to me? I fail to understand how it is possible to give the Lord full attention when we are alone, unless we know something of the real meaning of conscious worship.

In my not-too-long-ago-do-it-yourself approach to God, I congratulated myself on the fact of my daily faithfulness in having a Quiet Time. My spiritual temperature went up or down as I did or did not keep my Quiet Time. And when I spoke to others, I gave the impression that I always had a successful Quiet Time, and was, of course, always "victorious." This was far from the truth.

The truth, I am now joyfully discovering, is that even when I am false, He is true. I change, but He never changes. Have you discovered that no matter what you are like, He is always the same? His faithfulness is as certain as the law of gravitation. This discovery will turn your attention away from yourself to Him. And then, when you stop paying attention to yourself, you find that He is your victory. He is the Giver, and with Him come all the gifts that you have been seeking. They are all in Him.

Through all the years of my do-it-yourself period, with all my many attempts to "die to sin" I was still alive, and very much alive. Through all my sincere attempts to "abide in Christ" I was still too often expressing my own selfish spirit, and not His spirit of holy love.

And then I discovered — worship.

True worship takes place within the quietness of the individual. True worship is subjection to Jesus Christ. True worship depends upon the kind of God you worship. True worship is not conditioned by any religious atmosphere. It is like a well of water springing up from within the heart of the lover for the Beloved.

It took a negative form of worship to open my eyes to the meaning of true worship. I was visiting my first Chinese temple in the city of Shanghai. Inside, it was dark and shadowy and lined with double rows of dusty idols on heavy pedestals. At the far end was a tall loft and a giant gilded idol was set among heavy draperies that covered all but its feet. A Chinese woman came in to worship. She burned incense, she waved it before the dumb idol, she prostrated her little self before the huge fifty-foot god and waited for an answer. Was there any? There was none.

So that was "worshiping idols." Suddenly I knew that the God I worshiped was alive, that He was a Person who responded to me and to whom I could respond.

But did I worship the Ever-Living One?

Did I really know what worship meant?

Suddenly I wanted to get out of that temple and go home. I wanted to go into my own room and close the door and lock it. I wanted to get on my knees with my face to the floor, like that little Chinese woman. But unlike her, I wanted to worship the living God who created and sustains all life, and who has revealed Himself as He is in the Person of Jesus Christ. I wanted to be quiet and let all the love and adoration and worship of my heart go out to Him in a way that I had never done before.

Worship to me had meant "Sunday morning worship service." I wonder sometimes now what that means, for I have learned that it is in silence, holy silence, that my heart pours out its best love and worship to my Lord and my God. I have learned that worship is that honor, respect and adoration a small earthling like me can feel and give to the Almighty Creator.

My concept of worship has grown and deepened, and this is now the most important part of my Quiet Time. It is out of this personal worship that I find myself ready to share and be a part of a group of God's children.

In Part II of this book, you will find two devotional day-by-day studies. This material was prepared in booklet form for use with college students on the west coast, and is a simple, step by step devotional guide to personal worship. It is a study of God's character. Each day you will make use of what you learned the day before, and you will learn to worship.

It is when I am worshiping God that my heart is cleansed, that I am assured of His great love which has taken full responsibility for me. It is then that the Cross and the sufferings of

Christ awaken my heart to know more and more of the depth of His love. It is when I am worshiping and lost in wonder, and my conscious and unconscious self pours out love, that I become a whole person. It is when I have thus worshiped God that I begin to know the meaning of "Abide in me and I in you."

Before I grasped this truth about worship there was endless self-effort. Now it is a matter of resting in Christ.

CHAPTER 8

What Is Faith?

"I don't seem to be able to get answers to my prayers the way other people do. I wish I had that kind of faith!"

Have you ever said this? Until we begin to understand the laws under which faith operates, we cannot expect to make much progress. Understanding is knowledge, and knowledge is power.

Is faith a special gift which is given to some and not to others? What is the source of faith? Is it for all of us? Are God's answers given to those who possess faith, and withheld from those who do not have it? Can one know whether he has faith or not? Is receiving conditioned only by how much faith we have, or are there other important factors? Isn't it true that sin in our lives hinders God from answering prayer? And don't we have to exercise our faith so it will become stronger?

The answers to all these questions are found in the prayer promises which abound in the New Testament. They are also found in the gospel accounts of desperate men and women who made their way into the presence of Jesus Christ.

Mark records a miracle for us in the fifth chapter of his gospel which has helped me a great deal in understanding more about what faith is and how it operates. In this story there are five lessons which begin to unfold the mysteries of faith, the faith which asks and receives.

The first one is God's willingness to give us what we ask for. The second one is what to ask for. The third one is how to ask. The fourth is the important place "desire" plays in asking. The fifth is the necessity for a "point of contact."

1. God's Willingness

If you are not familiar with the story of the woman who touched the hem of His garment, turn to Mark 5:21-43 and read the whole story. Her healing caused an interruption in Jesus' journey to the home of an influential man with a critically ill daughter. And because of that interruption, the daughter was dead when they arrived. Jesus knew this beforehand, but still the true character of God was displayed in His love and kindness to the woman as well as to the distraught father.

Jesus Christ and the Father are One. Jesus is the Word, and "the Word became Human and lived a little while among us, and we actually saw His glory . . ." (John 1:14, Williams). God Himself is willing to be interrupted when He is on the way to meet the desperate need of Jairus, because He knows He not only can heal this sick daughter, He can raise her from the dead.

God is willing to give us what we ask for, even if it means a delay in His day's journey, and even if it means death at the end of the journey. He is willing to do this because of what He is like. He can handle one as well as the other. His eternal love and kindness and tender mercy go far beyond the care of an earthly father and mother. He is more willing to give than we are to receive. No eye has seen nor has any ear heard all the things that God has prepared for those who love Him. It was John Newton who wrote:

> Come, my soul, thy suit prepare:
> Jesus loves to answer prayer;

He, Himself has bid thee pray,
Therefore will not say thee nay.

Did you ever make a study of the prayer promises in the New Testament with the idea of finding out what God is like? I could copy these promises and fill several pages, but doing it yourself always brings surprises. Writing them down and looking at them helps you find words or ideas which are alike in all these passages. Here are some references,* but no doubt you will find many more in your own Bible concordance.

After such a study, one word seemed to light up for me. See if you can find it for yourself in this next paragraph which blends several promises.

All are freely invited to ask and to receive. We are told that we will receive what we ask for if we search and knock and ask. We are told to ask in Christ's name and He will do whatever we ask. We are told to abide (or to find our reason for living) in Christ, and then we can have whatever we ask for. We are also told not to doubt, and to believe that we are going to get what we have asked for.

In all of these promises the word that gets our attention is the little word "ask." Think what that means! God has told us *to ask* so that He may relieve the intolerable burdens of fear, tragedy and loneliness. The burdens of illness, poverty and injustice. God has told us to ask so that He may pour His gifts into our hearts and lives without measure.

If there is anyone who is not convinced that God is willing to give good gifts to those who call on Him, let that person finish this chapter before giving up.

Jesus was on the way to the dying daughter of a famous man when an unknown woman touched His clothing. He not only cured her, but He tenderly said, "Daughter . . . go in peace, be free from your disease."

There is no unwillingness in God to give. His eternal character is always on the side of love. It is only when our asking is out of

*Prayer References: Matthew 6:8; 7:7-12; 18:18-20; 21:21,22; Mark 11:22-26; Luke 11:9-11; John 14:12-14; 15:7; 16:24; James 1:5-8; I John 3:20-22, 5:14,15.

line with holy love that He withholds our answer. Withholding can be holy love, also.

2. What Shall We Ask For?

This brings us to our second point. What shall we ask for? And is there any special way of asking which will bring a sure answer?

Back to the sick woman in Mark 5. Did *she* have any difficulty in knowing what to ask? Certainly not. Well, you might argue, she didn't really ask, she just came up behind Jesus and touched His clothes. Yes, but coming and touching were her ways of asking.

In Mark 5 the woman's asking was in line with her need. For twelve years she had suffered as much at the hands of primitive doctors as from her hemorrhage. Her life was unbearable. She was on her way to an early grave. Then "she heard the reports about Jesus." I love that verse. "She heard the reports about Jesus." What reports? That whoever came to Him was healed! Look back or think back into the gospel records. When was anyone refused who came to Jesus for help of any kind? There was not one. Everyone who came received the help he asked for. Lepers were cleansed, blind eyes were made to see, demons were cast out and personalities restored. The lame walked, the deaf heard, the dead lived again.

This sick woman heard what Jesus had done and although her malady was not listed among the others, she was so desperate she decided within herself that if He could heal all those diseases, He could heal hers, too. *He* could do it. No one else. She was sure now, that *He was the one.* Her own desperate need drew her to Him, and if she could only get to Him, she would be well.

It was a glorious moment when I began to see that the power and authority of Jesus Christ were most often used when individuals, not crowds, asked for help. There were only a few whom He healed who did not ask personally. This too, shows His willingness and His knowledge of our needs.

What shall we ask for?

What Is Faith?

57

The simple answer is, *ask for what you need.*

3. How Shall We Ask?

What are your deep personal needs? Have you prayed about them? Have you asked the Person who can take care of them, to do it? Have you had your prayers answered? Or do you just grumble, and rebel, and blame other people?

Ask, says Jesus, ask largely, that your joy may be full (John 16:24).

How shall you ask?

When we look at the sick woman the answer to this question is simple, too. Ask in His presence. Get close to the Lord Jesus. Touch Him. He is the answer. He is my answer and He is your answer. He Himself is the answer.

"If you live in Me — abide vitally united to Me — and My words remain in you *and* continue to live in your hearts, ask whatever you will and it shall be done for you" (John 15:7, Amplified).

What does "if you live in Me" mean? It means that all my desire is centered in the Person of Jesus Christ, and apart from Him nothing permanently influences the real me.

How shall you ask?

In the dramatic account of her conversion story in *The Burden Is Light* Eugenia Price prayed only two words over and over from the depths of her heart and He heard. "Oh, God! Oh, God! Oh, God!" Her heart was so heavy there was nothing else she could do but call on His Name. It is not the actual words we pray, it is the condition of our hearts that brings the answer when we pray. In her case, as in all others, He Himself was the answer.

4. Desire

This brings us to the fourth point, desire. The sick woman in Mark's story had only one desire. A desire which had been a tiny seed of hope, and which grew through the reports which she heard about the healing power of Jesus. She believed that if she could get past all the obstacles and reach His side, she would be healed. Her need and her desire carried her past the forbidding obstacles of custom which kept women at home, and especially sick ones, lest they contaminate others.

How great is your need?

How deep is your desire?

Will it bring you to His side? Will it carry you past all that keeps you from Him? Will you stop what you are doing now, and kneel at His feet, in His presence? He is there. Ask, seek, knock. There *is* Someone on the other side of the door, and He will open it and give you all that He is. Christ and all His gifts are yours.

". . . the proof of God's amazing love is this: that it was while we were sinners that Christ died for us. If God is for us, who can be against us? He that did not hesitate to spare His own Son but gave Him up for us all — can we not trust such a God to give us, with Him, everything else that we need?" (Romans 5:8; 8:31,32, Phillips)

5. *Point of Contact*

Now we come to the last of our five lessons on faith, the necessity of a "point of contact."

What is a point of contact?

It is that very moment when you reach out and touch the hem of Jesus' garment, and you know you are healed.

Does living faith always have a person as a "point of contact"? Didn't the woman say that if she could but touch His clothing she would be healed? Wasn't it Jesus' garment that she touched? Yes, but was it Jesus' garment that healed her? Wasn't it rather the Person of Jesus Christ, and the power He possessed? He realized this, and that was why He embarrassed her by saying, "Who touched me?"

She had to tell her whole story anyway before the whole crowd. But Jesus had a good reason for this. Knowing human nature, He wanted to save her from the bondage which "experiences" or "relics" can have over us. Being a woman myself, I know what she might have done. She might have returned home looking for more symptoms, and even found them. And then she might have started out once more to find Jesus, this time with a small pair of scissors concealed in her pocket. She might have cut off a piece of His robe, so that she could touch it whenever she felt ill.

Jesus, loving her, and knowing the importance of a personal relationship, said to her, "Daughter, *your faith* [that is, your trust and confidence *in Me,* springing from faith in God] has restored you to health" (Mark 5:34, Amplified). He is the One we must all touch. Our hearts must climb that step of faith into His presence. He is already with us, and conscious of us. Climbing the step of faith is merely realizing that He is there.

If it is with another person that *you* can more easily climb the step to faith, and pray a faith-sized request, then you should plan to meet and pray with someone else.

This is where Matthew 18:19, 20 takes on fresh meaning. Certain things we seem to be able to ask for and receive when we are alone. Other things loom like great mountains, and we need the faith and prayer of one or two others to help us. "If two of you agree (harmonize, together make a symphony) about — anything and everything — whatever they shall ask, *it will come to pass and be done* for them by My Father in heaven" (Amplified).

Your point of contact is when you touch Jesus Christ, whether you are alone or with someone else. And your point of contact may be determined beforehand.

How does one find that point of contact? By asking, by praying, by being consciously with Him in prayer. Listen for His voice, the voice of the Shepherd who goes before His sheep. He will tell you. He is your first "point of contact." He will show you what to do next.

Our little sick woman in Mark's account had a point of contact, and who knows how long it had been in her heart? She would steal up behind Him, so no one would be embarrassed by her illness, so she would not have to tell what it was, and reach her hand through the crowd surrounding Jesus. When she *touched His clothing* she would be healed. She knew it beforehand. That was her point of contact.

Your point of contact may be that very moment at which two of you agree in prayer. It may be the moment the other person lays his hand on you and prays for you. It may be the moment you kneel at an altar of prayer. If you listen for the Shepherd's voice in your inner heart, He will tell you and He will lead you, and He will heal your heart or your body, for He is both able and willing.

Living faith is always in the Person of Jesus Christ. The Chinese word for faith, *hsin,* has several interesting root-characters. On the left side stands a man, on the right side is a small squarish opening out of which spring several short lines, denoting a mouth and the words being spoken. So then, faith is the confidence one has in a man and his words.

Do you believe in Jesus Christ? Then you have faith. Faith to ask Him for anything because you believe in Him. You will know what to ask and how and where, because you believe in Him and love Him. Your greatest need can be your greatest asset, for need is the golden door through which He comes close to His loved ones. Christ promised, "Lo, I am with you all the days, — perpetually, uniformly and on every occasion — to the [very] close and consummation of the age" (Matthew 28:20, Amplified).

Jesus Christ is our "point of contact," and as we touch Him, alone or with others, power is released and our prayers are answered.

CHAPTER 9

What Is Unanswered Prayer?

In this chapter we will look at the difference between unanswered prayer and obstructed prayer.

Is there such a thing as unanswered prayer?

Some people seem to think so, because recently I found this quotation: "Many of our prayers are not answered, and for this we should be grateful." In one sense, that is true. But whoever wrote that was speaking of the foolish and unwise things we are apt to ask for in our human ignorance.

I am sure the Lord, in His great loving wisdom, sifts all our requests, and the ones which might harm us are not answered according to our asking. Because of His care, all that may seem disappointing will bring some good. I believe this, because I am learning more and more about Him. God is greater by far than any idea or concept man could possibly conceive.

However, there are prayers which are "unanswered" because they are hindered. They could be answered, and some day they may be answered, but for the time being are held up by some obstacle. The heavy snows in Chicago held up morning traffic this past winter for six hours. But when colliding cars were hauled away and the snow plow got through, the flow of traffic went on.

Is there a chief obstacle which may hinder our prayers? Jesus mentions lack of forgiveness a number of times in references closely connected with prayer promises. The text doesn't really state plainly that unforgiveness will keep our prayers from being answered, but it is strongly implied. Jesus says, "When you stand praying, forgive . . ." and, "If you do not forgive, neither will your heavenly Father forgive" (Mark 11:25,26).

I'd like to mention three qualifying conditions for answered prayer in the gospel accounts. All of them are stated in the positive (but there is a negative meaning implied).

1. That we should ask in His Name (John 16:24).

2. That we should let His words live in our hearts (John 15:7).

3. That we should not be discouraged if we do not receive an immediate answer, and we should keep on asking, keep on knocking and keep on believing (Matthew 7:7,8).

Let us examine the meaning of these three conditions.

1. *In His Name* means "presenting all I AM" (Amplified). All of the character of Jesus Christ is set forth in His Name. This means all of the character of God. What we ask, then, should be in keeping with what He is like, and a request unlike Him cannot be granted.

2. To let His words live, or abide in us, as a condition for answered prayer, means that we let Him live right in our hearts. Jesus Christ is Lord. *He contains His words.* This is a vital union of two hearts, the one living within the other. Such oneness will produce a unity of purpose. So how could one ask for anything that was not right, pure and good?

3. To have our prayers answered, we must keep on asking, keep on seeking, keep on knocking. This is the continuing action of the Greek verb in Matthew 7:7, 8 and also of Luke 11:5-13. It is the story of the man who wanted bread at midnight, and kept asking until he received it. Don't give up. Don't get discouraged, keep asking. Why? The only reason I know is that prayer changes me because I am in His presence, and then I either begin to change my requests, or I become able to cope with my circumstances which may or may not change.

Actually there are no unanswered prayers in one sense, because if we ask for what we want in His Name, and we are living in Him, and we keep on asking, the answer will come. It may be yes or it may be no, but the answer is from God, and it will be His best.

We do understand, however, that some answers to our prayers are delayed. This is because God answers them in His way instead of in ours.

Hindered or obstructed prayer is a very real thing and is not the same as unanswered prayer. When we are not living in Christ or letting Him live in us, there is always a reason. John, in his first epistle (I John 3:21, 22) tells us that if our hearts are guilty because we are not watchfully observing His suggestions and plans for us, our guilty hearts will keep us from coming boldly to God. And our guilty hearts will keep us from asking and receiving what God wants to give us (Amplified).

This explains how unforgiveness or resentment toward another can hinder our prayers. Unforgiveness on our part automatically creates guilt in us. If I cannot love my brother whom I can see, how can I love God whom I cannot see? (I John 4:20) Love of God and love of our fellow man go together. *I will love God only as much as I love the person I dislike the most.* The kind of love God commands us to have is a genuine caring about what happens to the other person. It doesn't necessarily mean being attracted to him. It means caring about what happens to him.

So long as I am blinded by an unforgiving spirit toward my brother, how can I see God? There is blessedness for the pure in heart, for they see God. Lack of forgiveness is the equivalent of an impure heart. Resentment and unforgiveness are the roots of many diseases from which people suffer intensely. Only God can heal an unforgiving heart. Forgiveness is the ultimate proof of love — both of God's love and of our love to one another.

Love goes into action to make the first move. Love does not wait for the other person to come first. Love does not wait for the other person to take the blame and reach out first. These are some of the ways of love.

To be unforgiving is rebellion against God. He wants to forgive our sins, but Jesus says again and again that we must forgive others when we pray, so that our Father can forgive us our sins. To refuse to do this is rebellion. All rebellion is initially against God. All sin comes under that word, "rebellion." No matter what it is, it is some kind of self-assertion which is omitting God. Let's face it — this is sin. It is a defiance, open or secret, which resists the authority of Jesus Christ.

Rebellion is a real obstacle to having one's prayers answered. Sin is the only thing which hinders our prayers from being answered. And what will we do about it? What can we do? Confess our sins? Die to sin? Or carry with us a partial-condemnation all day long, day after day, because we are "not all that God wants us to be"?

I had a strong sense of rightness in going ahead with this chapter, because for many long impossible years I tried to be free from sin. I tried to die to sin. I tried to confess it all. I tried to believe it was all gone. Now, with great relief, I know I am a sinner *being* saved. I am not doing it myself. I have been saved, I am being saved, and I shall be saved. And He is doing it all. I know that Jesus Christ, by His death and by His life, is my righteousness.

I want to give you one of my favorite Bible verses on this subject, regarding what to do about sin in one's life. For me, this was the answer, and showed me how Jesus Christ is taking full responsibility for my life.

The Amplified New Testament is clear on Romans 5:10. "For if while we were enemies we were reconciled to God through the death of His Son, it is much more [certain], now that we are reconciled, that we shall be saved [daily delivered from sin's domination] through His [resurrection] life."

All the known or unknown rebellions of my life are being taken care of through the power of Jesus Christ's resurrection. I know, too, that He expects me to cooperate with Him in bringing my will under His control, so that all these rebellions can be stripped of their dominating power. When, face to face, I am alone with Him in prayer, and His love is pouring over me, somehow it is possible to hand over to Him the specific thing that I wished to manage myself.

And you, my tender-hearted, overly conscientious friend, can rest in Him, too, so that your prayers will be answered, and so there is no need to continue condemning yourself.

Who is he that condemns? Do you know the answer to that question? Do you condemn yourself? Oh, yes, you do, in a way that helps you turn positively to Christ. But the morbid, negative daily condemnation which is sapping your life and keeping you from receiving all He wants to give you, is wrong, because He has already died for you. The Christ who died for you and rose again is the only One who can condemn you. And He does not (Romans 8:31-39). He loves you. He loves you more than you are loved by anyone else in this world or in the next. God loves you. The Son of Man is come not to condemn but to save (John 3:17).

When you do find something that condemns you, bring it at once to His feet, and it will be transformed. Because all the fruits of the Spirit are sins transformed. Resentment is changed to love. Sadness is changed to joy. Unbelief is changed to faith. Rebellion is changed to acceptance. These are simply the gifts which accompany the Giver. Where He is, and where He lives, are all a part of the good things He wants to give to us. We don't pick faith out of the air.

Jesus Christ is our faith.

There is, of course, the possibility that you don't want to be changed in some area. That could really be an obstacle to your prayers, and they might have to wait some time for an answer. And yet, here again, God is so great and His love so strong that He knows why we balk at something. He lets us sulk or pity ourselves, while He in His eternal goodness keeps on giving and giving. Who can question Him? Who can say what He should do or what He shouldn't do? The fact remains,

> God loves all people.
> All people are sinners.
> Therefore God loves all sinners.

It is true no matter from what angle you approach it. God

loves you, as you are, in your rebellions, in your sins, and He loves you eternally. The proof of this was a Man on the cross, an historical fact, more than nineteen hundred years ago, and yet ever true. Because this Man lives today!

> *God so loved . . . that He gave*
> *His only begotten son . . .*

And he died for all, so that all those who live might live no longer to and for themselves, but to and for Him Who died and was raised again for their sake (II Corinthians 5:15, Amplified).

Keep on asking and it will be given you; keep on seeking and you will find; keep on knocking [reverently] and the door will be opened to you. For everyone who keeps on asking receives, and he who keeps on seeking finds, and to him who keeps on knocking it will be opened (Matthew 7:7, 8, Amplified).

CHAPTER 10

What Are Faith-Sized Requests?

What is a faith-sized request?

A faith-sized request is first of all a request which is just the right "believing" size for your faith. It is not a request which is so large that the very size of it makes you wonder if God will answer. It is a request for a particular situation, in which you pray for a special person or thing, and ask only for that which you can *really believe God will do.* This does not limit what God can do, but it honestly recognizes the size of your faith. There is every reason to believe that you will be asking for larger things as your faith grows.

Let me illustrate this by a prayer-promise in Mark and also by several true experiences.

> *Jesus . . . said to them, Have faith in God (constantly). Truly, I tell you whoever says to this mountain, Be lifted up and thrown into the sea! and does not doubt at all in his heart, but believes that what he says will take place, it will be done for him.*
>
> *For this reason I am telling you, whatever you ask for*

in prayer, believe — trust and be confident — that
it is granted to you, and you will [get it] (Mark 11:
22-24, Amplified).

The first thing the Lord tells us is to have faith in the One who
is able to answer. That is one of the lessons in faith which we
examined in Chapter 8. We are told that no matter what mountain
stands in our way, if we *ask and believe it will be moved, it will
be done.*

To ask and believe is the opposite of wondering in your heart
if you will receive it. That negative picture in your mind of "not
receiving" is doubt, and doubt will surely keep your prayer from
being answered. However, God has given us power over our
imagination, so by the positive use of that imagination, we can
picture ourselves receiving the answer. This is the way to believe
in one's heart, and to believe that he will receive whatever
he requests.

Jesus repeats this promise again in the next verse, and does not
limit it to any one mountain. He says, "*Whatever* you ask for in
prayer, believe . . . that it is granted to you, and you will get it."

Those are strong, positive words. There is no "if" or "maybe"
involved. Why is it then, that we don't ask for more? Why is it
then, that we seem to get so little when so much is needed?

About the time I began to be aware of honesty and simplicity
and brevity in audible prayer, I listened carefully when others
prayed, and also checked myself after I had prayed. I asked
myself these questions:

For what *definite* thing have I prayed?

Did I believe I would get it?

Did I picture myself receiving it?

The tragic answer was that I wasn't asking for anything definite,
and I wasn't receiving anything definite. I was merely praying
platitudes, "Lord, bless my family in America, and bless the Chinese pastors working in Shanghai, and bless . . . and bless . . . and
bless . . . ." The words bless and blessing do get a workout! But

what exactly are we asking for? Are we definitely asking for something? Are we talking to anyone? Are we expecting an answer from Him?

Two things began to appear in my short simplified prayers. I saw to it that I thanked Him for something, and I asked Him for something, no matter how small it seemed. At first, it was difficult to keep my prayers short, but I did it deliberately in order to make myself think specifically, and not just let words flow out without any thought back of them.

In the asking, I was careful to ask only for that which I believed He could do. If you think it is easy, try it, and keep your mind definite. The first thing I knew, I was editing my prayers. I would ask for something, and then quickly ask for forgiveness, because I found I didn't really believe I would get what I was asking for. Then I would try again. Finally I would arrive at one small request (compared to the first one) which I confidently believed God could do and would do in the given situation.

In my book, *The Years That Count,* I have illustrated this point in a detailed story in the 17th chapter. When Karen prayed for the conversion of her boy friend, Chuck, she was unable to believe he would be saved the first week, but she was able to believe that, on the very next date she could tell him about her own Saviour. She was enabled to do this. Then she prayed that he would accept a New Testament. He did. Then, that he would be willing to read it. He was willing. The story continues, until two weeks after her first request, Chuck made an open acknowledgment of faith in Jesus Christ.

Frequently, it is our experience to pray for the conversion of a loved one for years without an answer. That is not because God isn't willing to save the loved one. It is because we are not praying sensibly and with faith. It is like trying to take one giant leap from the bottom of the stairs to the top. We *want* to get to the top. We talk and talk about going and yet there we stand. We realize it is impossible to get from the bottom to the top of a flight of stairs in one step. Stairs were made to be used, but they must be used one step at a time!

The prayer of faith is similar. Climbing one step at a time is what we mean by a faith-sized request. Take one step at a time. Pray only for what you believe God can do in a definite situation, in a given time period.

To further illustrate faith-sized requests, I'd like to give you the experience of a married couple who moved into a new neighborhood. One of the first requests Mary and Jack made was, "Lord, we'd like to get acquainted with our neighbors, and if they don't know You personally as their Saviour, we'd like to introduce them to You."

That was an excellent request and right in line with what God wanted to do. But it was the description of a goal to be reached, not a step to take. They got down to business and took the first step.

"Lord," prayed Jack, "I'd like to meet the fellow next door and get acquainted. I'd like to begin today, and I believe You can help me. Thank You, Lord." Mary agreed with Jack in her prayer, and gave thanks with him.

The morning had scarcely turned to afternoon when the answer came. Their children got into a quarrel over a tricycle with the neighbor's children. Both fathers rushed to the scene. Jack took all the blame for his children, and put out his hand, "I'm Jack M., just moved in, glad to meet you." The first request had been answered. The first step had been taken.

The second step: "Lord, I'd like to know what that man is interested in, so we can become friends." The answer came within two days. He was interested in football.

The third step: "Lord, I need two complimentary football tickets, and may I have them by this weekend, please." The tickets came. The friendship grew.

The fourth step: "Lord, I'd like to invite my new friend to the Bible class I teach a few miles from here. Will You put it into his heart to accept when I ask him to go with me tonight?" He accepted. All the way over as they drove, they talked about football. All the way home they talked about Jesus Christ, and what it meant for Him to become one of us . . . God became a Man.

The fifth step: "Lord, Mary and I would like to invite my friend and his wife to our home some evening this week for a little talk and Bible reading together." The friends came — they read and talked quietly together.

The sixth step. "Lord, next week when I ask them over again, will You prepare their hearts, so that they will be ready to accept You as their Saviour? I believe this is the time to ask for this, and I thank You for all You'll be doing in the meantime to draw them to Yourself." When the next week came, the neighbors willingly and gladly accepted Jesus Christ.

This method also works in matters of guidance about getting a job, taking a trip, buying or selling a home, getting married, writing a book, or anything you may think of, be it small or large.

Another illustration: Last year at the Mound Keswick Conference in Minnesota, I met Rev. Harold De Vries, one of the speakers. We attended each other's meetings. My subjects were conversational prayer and faith-sized requests.

After returning to his church Mr. De Vries spoke to his people about conversational prayer. Sometime later the women of the church invited me to speak to them on the subject. Later, Mr. De Vries told a friend what was happening among a few groups meeting to pray conversationally.

"Why wouldn't it be a good idea for your people to meet in small groups and learn to pray like this?" his friend asked.

Mr. De Vries decided he would introduce the subject at the next Wednesday night prayer meeting. During the day he asked the Lord to send 150 persons to prayer meeting that night. Then he remembered "faith-sized requests," and asked himself if he really believed God could send 150 people.

He changed his prayer. "Lord, I believe You can and will send a hundred interested persons to prayer meeting tonight."

There were one hundred persons there that night, and they were all interested in forming groups to pray conversationally. By the next Sunday another fifty had signed up, making a total of 150. They are meeting regularly in groups of from two to six in homes, in offices, in the suburbs and in the Loop. The needs of the people are being met. Spontaneous prayer is offered for one another, faith-sized requests are being answered, more people are taking part, requests are being covered. There are fewer clichés, less padding, more honesty and simplicity in prayer. Men and women are coming close to God and to each other in the Winnetka Bible Church.

The wonderfully exciting thing about faith-sized requests when two or more are praying is that when you pray by subjects, exactly the same requests will come at the same time. That is when *faith* rejoices and cries, "It shall be done!" That is the moment when doubt disappears. That is when the whole mountain moves — or sometimes only half of it. But the other half will go, too, if you are willing to wait for the next step.

CHAPTER 11

When People Pray Together

The book, *Prayer Can Change Your Life,* by Dr. William R. Parker (Prentice Hall) is the story of an unusual experiment which applies the methods of modern psychology to the study of prayer.

By the use of three controlled groups, Dr. Parker and his co-author, Elaine St. Johns, were attempting to find out if prayer, rightly understood and practiced, would equal the treatment of psychotherapy.

For this purpose forty-five volunteers were interviewed and carefully divided into three groups of fifteen individuals each.

Group 1 was to be given the best psychotherapy possible in weekly individual counseling sessions for the purpose of remedying emotional disorders.

Group 2 was made up of the random pray-ers, who preferred neither the psychotherapy nor the prayer therapy. They were to pray alone every night during the nine months.

Group 3, the prayer therapy group, was to meet weekly for a two-hour session to talk and pray together.

All forty-five were given five recognized personality tests to determine what lay in the subconscious that might be a clue to the problems and disturbances in each life. The findings were also to act as a guide to determine progress at the end of the nine months.

In the prayer therapy group, a sealed envelope was handed to each individual once a week, which contained his homework. On this slip was written some undesirable emotion, discovered through the tests, about which he was to pray earnestly for one week; the next week he was told to forget about that one and was given another envelope and another piece of homework. There was no suggestion made that the contents should be shared, but soon the group voluntarily began discussing and sharing their own experiences and the progress they were making. Dr. Parker reports that *inhibitions and barriers crumbled as they recognized that each one needed the help and the healing and encouragement that came from sharing with the group.*

At the end of nine months, the tests revealed the following results:

Group 1. Those receiving individual psychotherapy with no mention of religion or prayer, showed 65% improvement, but each desired more treatment during the coming months.

Group 2. The random pray-ers, who prayed every night on their own showed no improvement at all.

Group 3. The prayer therapy group showed 72% improvement both in symptoms and tests, and the conclusive evidence of spiritual healing was indicated by the fact that *all of them wanted to help others as they had been helped.*

If you feel you need to be in a prayer group of this kind, you do not necessarily need to be in a controlled group such as Dr. Parker conducted. The story of what happened to the fifteen persons in the prayer therapy group has happened to many other groups who met and prayed with simplicity and honesty. It can happen to you and to your group. It isn't necessary that some certain person give you special lessons on conversational prayer.

It is necessary only that you thoroughly believe in the therapy of group prayer, as taught by Jesus Christ in Matthew 18:19,20.

There are no formal or rigid rules for conducting a prayer group. We come together first of all to pray, and to be conscious that we are in the presence of God, where we find spiritual hope and healing for all the ills of body, mind and spirit.

1. *How to Start a Prayer Group*

If you are *not* now connected with any group, and want to pray with someone, the Lord Jesus will help you. "Ask, and you shall receive." Start with one person. Send a copy of this book to a friend whose name will come to you when you pray. Find out later how he or she liked it, and suggest that you two meet together to pray. It is the Father who has made us members of His family, and it is His will that we find each other and learn to talk to Him together.

If you *are* connected with a group, share with one or two of the members your own personal prayer failures. Do this with kindness, and then discuss the remedy which you believe will be helpful. Share this book or another book on prayer. Read it aloud together, discuss it honestly, and then stop and pray. New habits will have to be formed and old ones discarded. This takes practice and concentration. The function of prayer is to set God at the center of your attention, to forget yourself and the impression you are making on others. As you open your heart (saying *I,* when you mean yourself, and *we,* when you mean all of those present) you will find God's love and joy healing you.

2. *The Place*

Because this is an informal kind of prayer, the place should also be informal. Not a large room or auditorium. Unless you can arrange the chairs in a circle in one corner, a small room is better. It should be a place where you will be undisturbed. Any possibility of disturbance will tend to check the ease and freedom of those praying, and interrupt the line of thought. If your children are screaming in the basement, you are probably used

to it by this time, but someone else may not be. Pray about
the location and the right answer will come.

3. *The Size of the Group*

The Michigan church about which I wrote in Chapter 6 started
their prayer meeting with twelve, with the idea of dividing as
the group grew. Since they are new at praying aloud, it is better
for them to stay together until a real love and union of hearts
has been reached through conversing with God. Then as their
hearts are open to Him who speaks to hearts, they will know
when and how they should divide.

In the Winnetka Bible Church (Chapter 10) the groups range
from two to six.

In Lima, Ohio, a large group meets in a home, and after sharing
and Bible study, groups of four and five go into almost every
room in the house to pray.

When the group is small, the members feel free to pray as
often as they wish. If the group is too large, someone is sure to
use it as an excuse to say to himself, "It doesn't matter if I don't
pray, the others will." Small groups may sometimes pray together as one large group. But the strength of any large group
is in the smaller intimate prayer groups who meet God face
to face.

4. *The Time*

Any time is the time for group praying. Any time when two
people can get together. A telephone conversation is a wonderful time to pray. You may feel self-conscious at first but that
will soon change.

The length of the prayer meeting will vary and will be determined, each time, by the needs of the group. I know of one group
of young people that spent most of the forty-five minutes in
singing, reading Scripture, giving requests, with only about five
or ten minutes for actual praying. After conversational prayer was

introduced, they reversed the program! Actually, this group of teenagers prayed one and a half hours the first time they prayed conversationally. They could scarcely believe it! They had enjoyed every minute and wanted more. That was because all of them were praying all the time.

5. The Position

Sitting around a table draws people together in a relaxed, intimate way. Sitting in a circle is also a favored position. Or kneeling by a sofa, or at an altar. Scattered seating is to be avoided. We are members of one family. And remember, don't pray into a sofa or a chair so no one can hear.

6. How to Make an Actual Beginning

a. Explain to your group what conversational prayer is, and why you want to pray this way. See outline on page 87.

b. Always remind yourselves, by a time of silence first, that you are actually in the presence of Jesus Christ. Act accordingly and prepare your heart in quiet worship. Don't be afraid of silence. He is there, and He speaks in a still small voice.

c. Then let someone open with a prayer of thanks that Matthew 18:19,20 is true. (That He is there with you. You have recognized His presence in your individual hearts in silence.)

d. Let others give thanks also, in sentence prayers. Give thanks first of all for the Lord Himself, for what He is like, for Himself alone. Then for His gifts: for eternal life, for some personal answer to prayer.

e. Let the "asking" or requests wait until everyone has joined one or more times in the thanksgiving. This may take a little reminding, as many people do not distinguish between worship and requests, between the Giver and the gifts.

7. How to Give Requests

Stating prayer requests to the group before you start to pray

78

can be a time-consuming and evasive practice. I well remember a meeting when the giving of requests lasted three times longer than the actual praying. It apparently is much easier to tell our problems to one another than to God.

The familiar "unspoken requests" can also be evasive, and tend to draw the person farther off into his or her lonely position.

As members of God's family (and members of the body of Christ) we are told to "bear one another's burdens." How can we do this unless we know the burdens others are carrying, and unless we make known our own burdens? "Bearing our own burden" could mean that the person who has the request upon his mind is the one who is to do the initial praying. Norman Grubb says that the man who has a definite desire or need is the man who has the faith to do the asking.

As soon as one has prayed about his own burden, another in the group should pick it up and pray, too, mentioning the person by name. This is what we mean when we say, "praying by subjects" (Chapter 3). Let as many as feel led by the Holy Spirit pray for this person until he or she is able to give thanks, or until there is freedom for someone else to introduce a new subject of prayer.

8. How to Agree in Prayer

Matthew 18:19,20 tells us to agree in prayer and we shall have an answer. How do we know when we have agreed?

Take the situation just mentioned. The person who made his difficulty known needs help. He may need some definite help. What is the next step he should take? Always ask yourself and ask the Lord, too: *What is the next step?*

When we pray together the Holy Spirit speaks to our hearts and suggests ways and means. When we are quiet and aware that we are in His presence, we are exercising love for one another. The "tree prayer meeting" in Chapter 3 is a good example of this kind of praying, but that is such a brief example. I've seen members of a group bear someone's burden until the same answer "was given" to several at the same time! And there was fullness of joy, just as Jesus Christ promised in John 16:24.

We agree that God's will be done. We agree by saying so when we pray. We agree that our brother will know the next step, even if it is doing nothing. Even if it is just waiting.

People who meet in small groups to pray usually begin to know each other well. We do not need to explain things to God in prayer (because He knows everything). We may come with confidence and ask with confidence. If you need to explain things to each other, stop praying for a moment and explain. Conversational praying is very natural, so whatever comes up, keep things natural.

When we don't know *what* to agree about, that is when the group goes into real Spirit-filled love action. We remind the Lord of His promises, we hold our brother's situation up in prayer, we mention his name, we lift together (each member perhaps doing one of these things). With our minds set together, we break through whatever darkness there is, or move whatever mountain there might be. We do this and believe we can do because Jesus Christ is present with us, and because we are asking in His Name, in His character and in His will. Asking in His Name means all these things. We converse in prayer, we suggest, we wait, we break in, we become aware, we stay in tune. (Conversation as defined in Chapter 3.)

9. *The Leader*

This subject was purposely left until number 9, so that no undue emphasis might be put upon it. He or she is only a chairman, or a moderator, not really a "leader." He should be sensitive, aware of the moving of the Spirit in the group, and of the brother or sister who needs that extra lift, which he can give by praying for him. As he feels moved by the Spirit, he can suggest various prayer subjects, examples of which will be listed in the next paragraph. However, don't feel that you must cover all these in one meeting. It is the work of the Spirit to guide. And it is a life changing experience to see how He does this through the honest spoken needs of various members of the group.

10. *Prayer Subjects*

Worship, thanksgiving, praise to God: the Father, the Son and the Holy Spirit.

Prayer for our loved ones.

Prayer for our own personal needs or projects.

Prayer for each other (i.e., ask each one to pray for the person to his right or left).

Prayer for your pastor and your church.

Prayer for those involved in a current newspaper account of a tragedy, etc.

Prayer for our nation, our statesmen, our missionaries.

11. *Silence — Pauses*

Someone has said, "Right prayer demands a quieting of the whole being." We need to learn to be quiet, and to be consciously aware of Jesus Christ. We cannot pray quietly if we are in a hurry. It is in the silences between prayers that He speaks to us, and our communion with Him purges and renews us. We should give audible thanks after such a time of silence. When no one is praying audibly, all should be praying silently, and should be so instructed. We are not there primarily to "get things" but to realize God's presence. This is the greatest answer to prayer — that we are consciously aware of the Great Shepherd and His unchanging love for us.

12. *How to Be Honest*

If no one in the group is willing to be honest there will soon be no prayer meeting.

The principle of honesty in prayer is twofold: First, that I say *I,* when I mean myself, and that I say *we* when I mean the whole group. The editorial "we" often is a substitute for honesty. Here is one version: "Lord, we ought to pray more often, and we ought to read our Bibles more often, forgive us."

Here is the other: "Lord, forgive me. I've read my Bible only once or twice this week, and I've just prayed on-the-run, and my heart is so hungry to be with You alone. Please forgive me. I put the controls of my day into Your hands."

The second principle of honesty is to pray where I am and not where I am not.

If I am struggling over hurt feelings for instance, I should say so, and do it without involving or blaming anyone but myself. It is dishonest to pray as though everything were fine and shining when it isn't true. If the matter is too personal to mention, you can still be honest enough to ask for strength to make a decision, or for grace to help in a certain situation. It has been said that "one gets it off one's chest by getting it on one's tongue." (See I John 1:9.) Honesty demands straightforward simplicity without apology.

Honesty goes right to the point!

13. *Difficulties*

a. *If one person prays too often.* I know from my own experience how eager one can become. Fortunately a friend took me aside and told me. "Wouldn't it be better if you waited a bit, to see if the Spirit might place the same request or the same answer in someone else's heart? Then you would have the joy of knowing that both of you were agreeing in the Spirit." It was much better. I became more aware of the need of others to express themselves, to take part in agreeing and thus fulfill the royal law: love one another.

b. *If one or more persons insist on long prayers.* This demands love and instruction. Perhaps first to the whole group, and then to the individual. Perhaps he or she will begin to pray shorter prayers as you pray and God answers. Long prayers tend to become impersonal and indirect, and when the group is praying conversationally, the others feel left out and unable to participate.

Try suggesting sentence prayers, or enough sentences to convey one idea only. If the person is new, someone should clue him before starting.

c. *If no one is praying an honest prayer.* Then you be that one. It will hurt. It may kill you. Kill your pride, that is. But it will bring rich abundant life. When God meets *you* in your honesty, someone else will realize a deep heart hunger to meet Him in the same way.

When the Holy Spirit is in full charge, there will be real freedom to pray honestly, sins will be forgiven and tensions released. The natural and expected result of prayer, in the Presence of God, is that healing love shall touch us all.

After all, prayer is conversing with God. To converse with someone we must be with that person.

And in His presence is fullness of joy.

Is This Your Story, Too?

Friend (who met me at the plane): "Our men's class is reading your book on prayer, and we are practicing conversational prayer."
Ros: "That's good to know. Now, I have a question. Are your men praying 'conversationally' on a common subject — or are they praying unrelated sentence prayers"?
Friend (after a brief silence): "Well, . . . I see what you mean. I guess we are doing the latter."

PART II
How to Have an Experience in Conversational Prayer

Introduction to Part II

When I was invited to speak to teenagers at two week-end conferences, I found that through their youth directors, John and Vel Shearer, they were already acquainted with the term: Conversational Prayer. Our program at those conferences consisted of: Three sessions in leadership training, four general lectures, small groups three times, with an evaluation session at the close of the week-end. (Mennonite Church. Headquarters: Elkhart, Ind.)

John Shearer wrote: "We just got wind yesterday of prayer groups that have been revitalized since Laurelville and Camp Tippecanoe experiences. One group in Ohio was surprised to find they had spent nearly two hours praying together! I've heard good experiences from many Ohio groups, as well as from our church college which was well represented at Laurelville. One college senior said he had had a break-through with a non-Christian friend since he's been practicing and talking about "God-loves-you."

Contents. Outlines on Conversational Prayer.

Chapters 1,2. Written by Vel Shearer for their teens.

Chapter 3. Teaching suggestions for chapters 1 & 2, using role-playing and group-evaluation.

Chapter 4. Vivid reactions of youth after the first time.

Chapters 5,6,7. More helps for you to get started.

Chapters 8,9,10. Daily Devotions and books to read.

Conversational Prayer

We Begin With His Presence

1. Jesus Is Here. . . . . Matt. 18:19,20

   Visualize Him. Use creative imagination and the
   Meditation card. Be silent. Be a little child at
   His feet. He loves you.

2. Thank You, Lord. . . . . Phil. 4:4-7

   Gratitude is worship which opens the heart.
   Be audible, brief, specific.
   Use open-end prayer, don't close it.

We Pray for Persons Present and Absent

Thus Receiving and Giving Love

3. Forgive me, Lord. . . . . James 5:13-16

   Confession is a part of worship. Be honest.
   Pray for yourself, then others will pray for you.
      This is prayer response.
      Say "I" when you mean yourself.
      Say "we" when all present can be included.

4. Help my brother. . . . . Mark 11:22-25

   Prayer-response should be audible, brief with
   love and thanksgiving. Use first names.
   The Holy Spirit will give you words when you pray.
   Give thanks when someone prays for you.
      This is agreeing in prayer.

This is Love in Action

Love one another as I have loved you. . . . . . . John 15:12
Ask whatever you will and it shall be done. John 15:7

This prayer from the heart is love in action. We become involved in God's purposes, in His view-point, and with each other's
needs. Then the circle will widen to include family, friends, church,
nation, the world.

(See pp. 89-93 for instructions.)

Meditation:

1. My child, I love you.

I love you unconditionally.
I love you, good or bad, with no strings attached.
I love you like this because I know all about you.
I have known you ever since you were a child.
I know what I can do for you.
I know what I want to do for you.

2. My child, I accept you.

I accept you just as you are.
You don't need to change yourself.
   I'll do the changing when you are ready.
I love you just as you are.
Believe this — for I assure you it is true.

3. My child, I care about you.

I care about every big or little thing which happens
   to you. Believe this.
I care enough to do something about it.
   Remember this.
I will help you when you need me. Ask me.
I love you.
I accept you.
I care about you.

4. My child, I forgive you.

I forgive you, and my forgiveness is complete.
Not like humans who forgive but cannot forget.
I love you. My arms are open with love.
Please come here! Come here to Me!
I forgive you.
Do not carry your guilt another moment.
I carried it all for you on the cross.
Believe this. It is true.

Rejoice . . . And Be Glad

(See p. 116 Fourth Day No. 1 for instructions).

CHAPTER 1

Never Heard of It?

by Vel Shearer

Really, it's nothing new. In fact, you may have participated in conversational prayer and weren't aware that it had a name. Let me tell you more about it.

You want to be loved and understood, don't you? Someone has said, "no man is an island entire of itself." He was right, and youth is no exception. God meant us to want to be with others. Conversational prayer is another way in which we can enjoy being together. Most important, Christ is with us. In fact, He becomes the center of our thoughts.

We talk to Christ together in an "ordinary conversation." Like any conversation, we may speak more than once. Of course, we don't make it up beforehand! We don't know exactly what we'll say or when we'll say it. We don't plan five minutes before, what we are going to say when we talk to one another.

Sometimes this kind of prayer is so honest it hurts. This spontaneous atmosphere keeps the conversation full of life and fresh. Planned, reheated, speech-style preaching-prayers are out!

Anywhere — in a car, at home, in a restaurant booth, in a buddy's bedroom, by a fireplace, by a window — just any place at all, we can "sit at the feet of Jesus" with three or four others and enjoy prayer. For prayer is enjoying friends and sharing what we know about Jesus Christ together. This is really having "refreshments" with joy.

Simple, isn't it? Next time you and your friends get together, why not make it meaningful? Suggest they try conversational prayer.

CHAPTER 2

Want to Tune in?

by Vel Shearer

. . . on a typical conversational prayer time?

Five teenagers from Rocky Ridge MYF decided to complete an evening of fun with conversational prayer around a friendly campfire. This is part of their prayer conversation: (A role-playing situation for you)

Sue: Jesus, thanks for being with us tonight.

Bev: It's great to have friends, Lord. Thank You for these Christian friends You have given me.

Sue: But Lord, help us to be friends to our buddies at school who aren't Christians.

Katie: Like Joey . . Father, help us . . to show her that real happiness comes as we serve You.

Bev: Help her to see that it is not boring to be a Christian.

Sue: Lord . . . help Joey to give herself to You. Show her that she must accept You as her Saviour. May she see by our lives that You give her peace. (There was a short silence, a relaxed silence, as the girls thought about Joey, and how much Jesus loved her. This is a way to pray, too.)

Muriel: Forgive us . . when we haven't done our part in being friends to Joey.

Sally: Father . . . like the time I didn't speak to Joey . . because she had cheated on the Math test. Forgive me, I guess I thought I was better than Joey.

Katie: Help Joey to see that we love her even though we don't like everything she does.

(another silence)

Bev: Tomorrow night is cleaning at Widow Brown's for our MYF-ers. Thanks, Jesus, for this opportunity to help someone You love *(aside)* and whom we ought to love too.

Sue: Thanks, too, for the new fellows who came last time when we cleaned the Gordon house after the fire. Bless Mrs. Brown, and her children without a father.

Katie: Please help her son, Tom, to be able to finish his year at school. Somehow help him to get enough money to pay his tuition . . .

Muriel: And thanks, Lord Jesus, for . . .

Question: How long should we go on?

Answer: As long as you want to.

Question: What about requests?

Answer: Make them up as you go along. Most of them you can pray about instead of talking about them. Try it and see.

Question: Can I stop and tell the group something, if I remember it then?

Answer: Certainly. Just say, "I've got something to tell you all . . . ." This is relaxed *conversational* prayer.

Question: You mean . . . . you can add to someone's prayer? or say "I agree too" or "That's my prayer too" ??

Answer: You certainly can, and should. This agreeing is Jesus' idea: Read Matthew 18:19,20. It helps our faith to grow, when we put these positive thoughts into words.

Want to Tune in?

91

CHAPTER 3

Did You Notice?

Learning, sharing and observing.

It is important that fresh impressions be shared immediately after introducing *Want to tune in?* Role-playing is a powerful teaching technique. It makes deep lasting impressions which need to be talked about, to incorporate them into daily personal living.

Questions will help the group open up and evaluate.
1. What did you like about that kind of praying?
2. How was it different from the old way?
   Subjects which will be mentioned. (See also Chapter 4.)
   Let them tell you, don't you tell them!
   Number in the group
   Where it was held.
   Length of time used.
   Length of individual prayers.
   Times each person prayed.
   Subjects which received attention.
   Definite or indefinite requests.
   Specifics: names, etc.
   Language used.
   Any time for wandering thoughts?
   Attitudes necessary: K.I.S.S.
   (keep it simple, stupid)
3. **Why not try it for real — right now?**

The above are guidelines for anyone teaching Conversational Prayer.

CHAPTER 4

Teens Tell What They Liked
(about conversational prayer.)

This is a new approach and I like it.

I received a new awareness of the Presence of Christ.

The thing that impressed me was that God loves me unconditionally.

Praying like this (dialogue) made me so aware; I've been half-
asleep most of the time.

Now I can pray to Jesus and not be afraid of what others will think.

With the new things I've learned, I want to go back to our church
and help get the formality out of our MYF.

I'm going to take that book *(Prayer-Conversing With God)* home
for others to read.

Also see pp. 124-126 for more reactions.

───── ╫ ─────

Pages 87 and 88 may be mimeographed. Give credit to author, book-title, publisher.
Send one copy to Ros Rinker, c/o ZONDERVAN PUBLISHING HOUSE, Grand Rapids,
Mich. 49506.

CHAPTER 5

Lucie Asks How

Dear Miss Rinker:

I have read two of your books and they are dynamic. Last year Jesus became alive and real to me in a *Faith At Work* conference in Birmingham, Alabama. Later I became an active member of a prayer group. I loved every minute of it!

Now I'm home and I'd like to start a group in my home. How can I know God's will in things? People here don't pray together, and they don't know about conversational prayer either. I know one thing: You don't have to tell people exactly what to do, you just tell what happened to you and give thanks.

Dear Lucie,

That was a great idea, and I'm sure you'll find it was really God speaking to you. How can we know? We don't always know for sure *before,* but afterwards we do, by the way things turn out.

1. Start with two or three and make a standing circle of love (hold hands, it helps). Then lead them in the Four Steps (see

"Conversational Prayer" — page 87). Make it short, easy, relaxed and personal. Sit down and talk about what you did.

2. You might read Chapter I of Part I, and talk about that.

3. You could ask: Shall we do this again? Read Chapter 2 and talk about that. Do the Four Steps again.

4. Keep the same few persons for a while, so they learn to trust one another, and to pray aloud in words — without fear. It's real exciting, and it grows on you. After you invite more persons (be sure they understand as you tell them what you are doing) break into circles of four to pray — it's easier that way. Especially when you come to Step 3, remember to be honest and pray for yourself and let others pray for you.

5. Always remember that First Step: Jesus is right there. Count on that. See Him in your mind's eye. Pray for each other by name. Always give thanks for *everything*. Keep it going in dialogue style.

6. You can pick up later suggestions from many sources. Just keep your eyes open, and your heart open to the Holy Spirit — for He is your teacher.

CHAPTER 6

A Teacher Asks How

Dear Ros,

How do you teach youth in today's world — to pray? They seem so different from us as we were growing up. H.C.

The Answer, from another adult:

Jane E. answers from her experience. She was a new Christian when I met her in Honolulu, and she attended my classes there. Quickly she put into practice what she learned, with her family and her teens in church-school.

"I have found that the youth in our church responded to prayer teaching much more quickly than the adult women in my circle. The Jr. Hi's are so open, especially if no stranger is present. The other day we asked God to heal four persons:

1. Jess, in our class, had a broken leg.
2. Our pastor was in an auto accident.
3. A neighbor (Lutheran) wasn't expected to live.
4. One of the grandmothers had an eye operation.

"It was so meaningful, because in all the above cases, we prayed briefly, knowing God loved each one, knowing God's power to heal, praying for the doctor on the case, and giving thanks for their healing."

Another letter:

Dear Ros,

I am a Sunday school teacher of seven, average age 16, and I would like to teach them to pray and to share in a personal way. I realize our first session must be interesting or they won't be willing to try it again. Any material you can send me will be greatly appreciated.

My Answer:

I sent her a copy of Vel Shearer's article: (see Part II chapters 1 & 2) and also the outline cards: Prayer-Conversing with God, and Meditation, found on pages 87 and 88. I also asked her to read any of my books she could secure, and begin to use and practice instructions given there . . . *with love.* To give instructions without love, in teaching prayer, is a sin against my brother.

The author's book, *Teaching Conversational Prayer.* (Word, 1970) will provide valuable and practical suggestions and exercises.

A Teacher Asks How

CHAPTER 7

Ros Answers Questions

So you want to teach someone to pray?

Or, you want to learn to pray yourself . . . with others?

All the material in this book is designed to correct wrong attitudes, to provide positive attitudes, to give you a new look at prayer with a fresh approach . . . . because God loves you, and because you learn to love one another (in truth) when you pray together.

Turn to the section on *Growth Through Reading,* and secure some of those books; they will give more specific help.

Question: Should teenage boys and girls be in the same prayer group?

Answer: Not when they are learning, but *after* they've learned how, it is good to mix them sometimes. You will find they are more relaxed, without fear, when they are in all-girl, or all-boy groups. Why? Because they are very self-conscious in each other's presence. They fear they might accidentally say something the boy-friend or girl-friend would not understand; they might leave the wrong impression, or their chances (for dating) might be hindered.

Question: How about Juniors?

Answer: Put the Juniors together, this works fine as they haven't started dating yet . . . some of them at least!

Question: What do you do with giggling girls . . . when you are trying to teach them to pray?

Answer: At their age, everything is funny, everything embarrasses them. Not necessarily ha-ha-funny, but in their eyes it is: we-like-it kind of funny. What to do? Help them. They can't stop unless you help them. Here are two ways:

1. "Well, girls, go ahead, we'll all laugh and then we can go on." They look up, laugh again, shift their feet, and then you go on as if nothing happened. Just stop and talk when necessary, or instruct.

2. In your prayer, as leader, say: "Well, thank You, Lord, for all this joy and fun we're having." (I really prefer the first way.)

Question: What if there is one big class or group of only girls? How is it best to divide them?

Answer: Dividing them into smaller groups helps them to overcome the fear of praying aloud. Divide them according to grade, or age. Freshmen girls in one group, Sophomores in another, etc., according to their loyalties, this seems to help. They already know and care about each other, and this break-down helps them to be honest. I've seen amazing things take place in such groups.

Question: What does one do if there are too many to teach, too many to divide into groups?

Answer: Have a pilot-leadership class and invite the youth who seem able to lead or teach others. They can do it! I've often handled it like this, and thus leave behind (when I'm on tour) those who have had training.

Illustration:

I recall an Ohio group of about 40 teens, half of them Methodist and the other half Presbyterian. We all stood in a circle, and I taught them the Four Basic Steps. We prayed together for about 15 minutes. In that brief time, all of them offered short, personal, honest prayers — many invited Christ into their hearts. Afterwards, I learned by telephone, the Methodist group stopped in a certain home and continued their praying until everyone in their group had accepted Christ. They loved every minute of this down-to-earth, joyous, Jesus-present approach to prayer.

Prayer is: accepting the unconditional love of God for yourself, and learning to love each other.

How to start a group:
See following pages:
76-83 practical suggestions
24-28 around the big tree
87   memorize this outline
89-92 dramatize this group experience
94,95 Lucie uses this book
96-100 Suggestions to a teacher

CHAPTER 8

How to Start Having Daily Devotions

This sample three-day study will help you get started on a life-long habit. It is prepared for use at home or at week end conferences for young people in ages ranging from 15 to 26.

Suggestions: Read once more the four pointers given in Chapter 7, Part I. Read only one day's lesson at a time, and don't pay too much attention to the time given there (five minutes, fifteen minutes, etc.). It is better to start with only five minutes than none at all. Young believers need the discipline of a definite time and place. Older believers who have learned the art of "praying without ceasing" (an attitude) still need a time to worship and to read the Word of God.

Daily Quiet Time
Three days

Purpose: The following pages contain a sample Quiet Time for those who have never settled down to a daily, regular devotional time, and who wish to make this a part of their Christian lives.

Suggestions: If you wish to do this three-day study, read again the four pointers for the Quiet Time in Part I, Chapter 7. Read only today's lesson. Keep each day's material fresh for the day on which you wish to use it.

Time: About twenty minutes for each study.

History: These three devotional studies were originally used at weekend conferences for young people ranging in age from sixteen to twenty-five. The pages were handed to the cabin counselor, who then made personal contact with each one during the day, as a follow-up procedure.

First Day

I. MEETING WITH GOD

Meditation: Time 3 minutes.

My Purpose: To meet Jesus Christ, my living Lord. To be quiet, and put all other thoughts out of my mind.
To say to myself, *He is here.*
To welcome Him, and to be glad.

II. TALKING WITH GOD

Prayer: Use these thoughts to make your own prayers. Time 5 minutes.

1. To give thanks means: To be grateful. Think of all you have to be grateful for, in your past, in your present. For the knowledge of God, of Jesus Christ, of the Holy Spirit. Be grateful for the Giver as well as His gifts.

2. To give thanks: For the pleasant things and the things that hurt you and cause you to suffer. Jesus suffered for us. He knows. Give thanks.

III. LETTING HIM TALK TO ME

Bible reading: Time 15 minutes.
My opening prayer. Psalm 119:18. Memorize it.

1. John 1:1-18. Study verses by reading more than once. Read quietly, thinking of the meaning. Read it again, aloud, to yourself.

2. John 1:1-4. For specific study.

a. Who is "the Word"?. . . . .

b. Write out verses 2, 3, 4, and put the name you wrote above in place of the pronoun "he" or "him." If you have the correct name, this will make good sense.

c. Who made the world and all of us?. . . . .

d. Make a list of the other names by which He is called in verses 1-18.

IV. QUESTIONS   Yes   No

1. Can one inherit Christ from one's parents?   . . . .

2. Do you have a friend who is a real
   Christian?   . . . .

3. Have you ever definitely accepted Christ
   as your Saviour?   . . . .
   When and where?. . . . .
   Do it now.

Second Day

I. MEETING WITH GOD

Meditation: Time 3 minutes.

My Purpose: To meet God face to face and worship Him.
            To give thanks and learn to worship.
            To learn to be quiet and alone with Him.

II. TALKING WITH GOD

Prayer: Make your own prayers including the above thoughts,
        as well as the following:
        Time: 5 minutes.

1. To worship God: Worship means that honor and respect and attitude of adoration that a small earthling like me can feel and give to the Great Almighty Creator, who is God and Saviour.

2. Think on the above sentence. Break it down, think on the meaning of each word, each phrase. Then remember He wants your worship (John 4:23,24), and start over again, and give it to Him, consciously being aware that He is there. Use words and use thoughts in your heart which you can't even put into words. Worship the living God who loves you.

III. LETTING HIM TALK TO ME

Bible reading: Time 15 minutes.
Prayer: Psalm 119:18. Pray it.

1. John 1:19-51. Give thanks for all you learned yesterday about "The Word." Ask to be taught by the Holy Spirit today.

2. Read aloud all of these verses. Time yourself, read slowly, and think of the meaning.
How long did it take you?. . . . .

3. On the sheet you used yesterday, continue the list of names used in this chapter for Jesus. How many do you have now?. . . . .

IV. QUESTIONS

1. Do you think that Jesus Christ is God?. . . . .

. . . .

How to Start Having Daily Devotions

105

2. Why? Write your answer. . . . .

. . . .

. . . .

. . . .

3. What made these disciples believe on Him?
   Write your answer. . . . .

. . . .

. . . .

. . . .

Third Day

I. MEETING WITH GOD

Meditation: Bring your thoughts to Jesus Christ.
Be consciously in His presence.

My Purpose: To worship Him.
To thank Him.
To let Him speak to me.
(Use thoughts of the other lessons.)

II. TALKING WITH GOD
1. To confess my own sins and needs in simple everyday language, and to accept and thank Him for His forgiveness and new life.

2. To pray for others: my friends and my family. He loves and cares for them, too.

106

III. LETTING HIM TALK TO ME

Bible reading: Time 15 minutes.

Prayer: Psalm 119:18. Pray it.

1. I John, chapters 1 and 2. Read these short chapters aloud.

2. Make a list of all the things you can find in these chapters
that Christians should do.

3. Make a list of all the things Jesus Christ does for "little
children" who belong to Him.

IV. QUESTIONS

Write down some of the things you have liked about this
three-day meditation, the things which have helped you most.

Further Suggestions:
Read pages 101 and 102 again. Take your hymn book with
you into your Quiet Time, and meditate and think upon the
words which inspired the writers: "When I Survey the Wondrous
Cross," "What a Friend We Have in Jesus."

How to Start Having Daily Devotions

CHAPTER 9

How to Go on Having Devotions

Purpose: A seven-day devotional study designed to lay a foundation in personal worship, through the study of some of the characteristics (or attributes) of God. The material is cumulative and progressive. Each day you will be using what you learned the day before.

Suggestions: It would be well to refresh your mind regarding the meaning of worship, by reading again the last half of Chapter 7.

Use the Introductory Lesson, as your first study. Please do not read tomorrow's lesson. Keep each lesson fresh for that day. Please try carefully and slowly to follow all instructions in order to gain the maximum good. These you will find sometimes so simple that only by doing them can you understand why they are of any value.

History: This material was originally prepared as Aids to Personal Worship, and used in month-long camps, first for teenagers, and subsequently for adults. The material has been tested and proven of inestimable value in teaching personal worship.

INTRODUCTORY LESSON

1. My motive: To meet Jesus Christ, my living Lord.

2. My preparation: Each night as you drop off to sleep, pray that you may awaken with real expectation and readiness to arise and spend the first freshness of the day with Him.

3. The place: Find a place to be by yourself, where your face is toward Him alone. This is important.

4. The books: Try one of the newer, modern translations of the Bible, as well as your favorite Bible. Take a hymn book with you.

5. Learn to use the hymn book as a means of worship. The hymns you do not know will become familiar friends as you read through the verses and worship your Lord.

6. Apart from the fixed and resolute determination of your will to meet Him, you will find it impossible to do this daily. Your will, mind, heart and body are involved in worship.

MEDITATION:

True worship is subjection to Jesus Christ.

Our Lord seeks worshipers (John 4:23). True worship comes from those who are His sons. Let us worship whether we feel like it or not. Christ is worthy to be praised for WHO HE IS, and for what He has done, and for what He is doing.

DEFINITIONS FOR DEVOTIONAL STUDY

Worship . . . that honor, respect and adoration a small earthling like me can feel and give to the Almighty Creator.

How to Start Having Daily Devotions

109

Praise . . . to glorify God in worship. To speak and sing of His Person, and of His works. To give thanks.

Glorify . . . to make wonderful and great by the love and devotion of my whole self to . . . God.

Confession . . . to be willing to face honestly my own sins and sinfulness, and to put it into words.

Petition . . . to ask the Lord for whatever I need for myself.

Intercession . . . to pray for others, as I pray for myself.

Meditation . . . to think quietly about the Lord, turning over in my mind what I am reading, and letting it sink in.

Thanksgiving . . . to be grateful and show it. Not only for the gift received, but for the Giver. Be grateful and be thankful.

"Come to me . . . . Learn of me."

First Day

MEDITATION

1. Enter His presence with expectation. "I am going to see Him, to meet Him!"

2. Humbly prostrate yourself. "He is the Great God, I am His child!"

3. Words are not necessary all the time. Just these silent thoughts and others like them. Take one of these, repeat it over and over until the full meaning begins to take hold of you.
   "He is the great Eternal yet I can approach Him."

4. Wait. Be silent. Be reverent. Keep your mind on the above thoughts. Draw near remembering the blood of Jesus Christ, His Son, makes you clean.

HYMN
"Great Is Thy Faithfulness"
1. Read it. Sing it aloud. Choose another on the same subject if this one is not in your hymnal. Find out what it says about Him.

2. Select one verse. Underline the parts which describe our God.

3. Compare His faithfulness with yours. Confess your need.

4. Give thanks and praise to Him, now. Use the words of this hymn. Praise Him.

BIBLE READING

Ask the Holy Spirit to open your heart.
Memorize Psalm 119:18.

Read	Names of God	His Characteristics
1. Numbers 23:19.		
2. James 1:17.		
3. Hebrews 13:8.		
4. Deuteronomy 7:9.		
5. Psalms 145:13.		
146:5,6.		
6. Psalm 91:4.		

How to Go on Having Devotions

TESTING

The following words describe the central truth I learned about our God in this lesson.

. . . .

PRACTICAL

Take with you all day these words and the ideas they convey. Recall them as many times as you can, with thanksgiving. This God is with you. Always. He loves you.

•   •   •   •   •   •   •

Real worship depends upon the kind of God you worship.

Second Day

MEDITATION

1. Using the instructions of yesterday, wait in His presence . . . until your heart and mind are very quiet. Quiet. Very quiet.

2. Remember . . . praise and worship belong to our God. (Review your definitions p. 109-110.)

HYMN

"Holy, Holy, Holy"
1. Sing it with your whole heart . . . remembering you are there before Him . . . offering your worship in song, in truth. Before His holiness I realize my unfitness . . . seeing Him, I am aware of my need. Yet, He bids me come . . . He accepts me because He is one with God.

PRAYER — Conversing With God

112

BIBLE READING My prayer: Psalm 119:18.

1. Read Psalm 46. Go through it again, aloud.

2. Read it as though the whole world is listening and you are proud to belong to such a God.

> Pause to give thanks again.

> Pause to confess your own sinfulness
> before His pure holiness.

3. Turn to the Book of Revelation. Read of the holiness of Christ. Take your place . . . in imagination with the great throng and sing with them.
Read the descriptive parts silently, and read the *praise* and *adoration* aloud.

Revelation 1:5-7)   Keep
Revelation 4   )   your attention
Revelation 5   )   upon the Lamb.

TESTING

From your reading today, write down the words that describe

the Lord, your God:. . . . .

. . . .

PRACTICAL

1. *Give* thanks that through the Cross and Resurrection of Jesus

How to Go on Having Devotions

Christ, you are made right . . . in His sight . . . that His holiness is yours for today's needs. He is your holiness.

2. *Share* with one person today what your Quiet Times so far have meant to you. Be specific.

• • • • •

Accept yourself as being sinful. To meet God is to cry out, "Depart from me, for I am a sinful man!" To meet God is also to cry out, "Thank You, LORD, because You have already taken full responsibility for me and my sin — forever!"

Third Day

MEDITATION

1. Enter His presence . . . with PRAISE. He loves you. He wants to let His love pour over you . . . like warm sunshine. Open . . . open and just rest. Rest and wait in His dear presence. Use the ideas (and notes) of the past two days.

2. On your knees. Call Him by all the names with which you are familiar. Repeat them . . . with love and adoration.

3. Let your WORSHIP be sometimes *silent,* with your whole being just going out toward Him; sometimes *vocal,* with just broken phrases, half-sentences, repeating His Name . . . for He is worthy.

4. Spend five or ten minutes in meditation. Do not leave until His love has warmed you, touched you, transformed you. Remember, HE LOVES YOU. His love meant . . . His death.

HYMN

Choose one of these, or a similar one:

"The King of Love"
"Jesus, I Am Resting"
"O Love That Wilt Not Let Me Go"

Read it, sing it, think of the meaning.

Underline the words describing His love.

Try "praying through" the words, making them your prayer
while you are singing.

BIBLE READING

1. Write out Romans 5:8:. . . . .

. . . .

Circle the important words. Pause to thank God for the real
revelation of Himself in the wonderful Person of our Lord
Jesus Christ.

2. I John 4:7-21. Read these verses. Form the habit of reading
alone and aloud. Try it now.

What word is repeated here? How many times?

Meditate on the source of love . . . the progression . . . from
whom to whom.

List the characteristics of love, as found in God:

. . . . ; as found in you:. . . . .

TESTING

Is there any person you will meet today to whom you can show the kind of love Jesus showed on Calvary? With forgiveness and gentleness, pray for him now. Love him . . . now. Seek him out today. Show LOVE.

•   •   •   •   •   •   •

The first step in worship is learning to be alone with God.

Fourth Day

MEDITATION Turn to page 88.

1. Read it. Now read it as if Jesus were saying those words to you. Read it again, whisper it, on your knees. Believe every word.

2. Draw near . . . and let your whole being desire His presence. See how many of the things you have just read can be recalled and quoted without looking.

3. Ask the Holy Spirit to teach you the real meaning of worship. Just ask Him . . . as you remember the words you have read.

HYMN

Choose a hymn, or select one of the following:
"Jesus Loves Me"
"When I Survey the Wondrous Cross"
"Hallelujah, What a Saviour!"

1. Read it aloud, slowly. Pray and praise with the author. Visualize the word pictures.

2. Find a few new expressions from this hymn to add to your growing list of praises with which you may adore your Lord.

PRAYER — Conversing With God

116

BIBLE READING

1. Isaiah 53. Keep in mind that all this suffering was because He loves you.
Read the chapter, remembering the phrase from the hymn, "Thou hast loved us unto blood."

2. Read Isaiah 53 again, aloud. Have you learned to pray and read aloud yet? Our living Lord is there with you. Speak to Him. Share with Him.
This suffering Saviour of Isaiah 53 is the same glorious Lamb of God who receives our praises in the Book of Revelation.

PRACTICAL

Spend some time in prayer today. Your growing love for your Lord means more love shown to your fellow man.

PRAY for your daily companions by name.

PRAY for members of your family by name.

PRAY for those you work with by name.

PRAY as the Holy Spirit leads you.

•   •   •   •   •   •   •

WORSHIP is meeting the living God and having my life changed by His presence, and by His love.

Fifth Day

MEDITATION

Enter His presence with anticipation and praise.

He is here.

Worship Him in spirit and truth.

He is faithful, never-changing.

Holy, holy, holy! Lord God of Hosts!

Loving, faithful, Holy God! My Lord!

> *Lamb of God, my soul adores Thee,*
> *While upon Thy face I gaze.*
> *Here the Father's love and glory*
> *Shine in all their brightest rays.*

Pause. Wait. Be still. Think on the meaning of each of the above words as you say them.

Use parts of other hymns to voice your praise.

HYMN

Choose a resurrection hymn, perhaps one of these:

"Thine Be the Glory, Risen, Conquering Son"

"Christ the Lord Is Risen, Today"

1. Notice to whom the hymn is addressed. Read it aloud.

2. Sing it, learn it if it is new.

3. Worship the Lord with this hymn.

BIBLE READING

1. John 19:19-31. Read it and see our Lord Jesus as the disciples saw Him at that time.

PRAYER — Conversing With God

2. Psalm 33. Observe carefully all that He has done by His great, great power.

PRACTICAL

1. Make Psalm 33:18-22 your own prayer, by rewording the pronouns. Use the first person. "Behold, the eye of the Lord is upon *me*." Read it several times like this, adding your own requests, and enlarging them as the Holy Spirit puts them into your heart.

2. All your personal private prayer should be in the first person. We are talking to One who is a Person, and One who is alive forevermore.

PRAYER

For others by name.

Share today's plans with your Lord, and talk over all the details with Him.

• • • • • • •

Worship is the response of my whole self to God.

Sixth Day

MEDITATION

Spend at least 10 minutes, including the hymn, in meditation. By this time you have many ways to worship your Lord.

Confess your coldness (when you feel that way), for this is being honest as you pray.

"Come to me . . . learn of me . . . and ye shall find rest." Let your heart pour out its silent gratefulness.

From the world of sin and noise,
      And hurry I withdraw;
For the small and inward voice
      I wait with humble awe;
Silent am I now and still,
      Dare not in Thy presence move;
To my waiting soul reveal
      The secret of Thy love.

                            — CHARLES WESLEY

HYMN

Choose one yourself for today. Choose one which expresses praise and worship to Christ.

BIBLE READING

Ephesians 1:15 — 2:10

Yesterday we read and thought about the power of our God, in creation, in becoming a man, in the resurrection.

Today we want to see how that power operates in us, what that power does to us and in us.

God's power in us

PRAYER

As your conception of the greatness of our God grows, your faith will reach out in prayer for your friends. Pray for them by name.

". . . the immeasurable greatness of His Power in us who believe.

120

. . . the immeasurable riches of His grace in kindness toward
us in Christ Jesus."

Seventh Day

Your meditation will usually consist of one or all of these
WORSHIP . . . out of which proceeds
     PRAISE
         CONFESSION
             PETITION
                 INTERCESSION
                     THANKSGIVING
My voice shalt Thou hear betimes, O Lord:
     Early in the morning
          Will I order my prayer unto Thee
          And will keep watch.

HYMN

Choose your own hymn.
Why did you choose it?
What did you find in it?

BIBLE READING

Psalm 139

First Reading: To get the general meaning and to open my
                 heart for instruction by the Holy Spirit (John
                 14:26; 15:12-15).

Second Reading: To notice all that is said about me, and God's
                 knowledge of me.

Third Reading: List all the characteristics of the Lord God
                 as stated or implied in this psalm.

Be honest to the last detail.

This is the key which restores and maintains real fellowship between my Lord and me. Treat yourself to the luxury of real honesty in prayer. He knows it anyway, but He longs for you to be honest, for then you can hear Him speak to you. Have you learned to recognize His voice? (Proverbs 8:32-36; John 10:3,4)

•　　•　　•　　•　　•　　•

True worship is subjection to Jesus Christ.

•　　•　　•　　•　　•　　•

For your next lesson:

On one of the blank sheets at the back of this book, write all the definitions (words, phrases, sentences, ideas) of "worship" you can find in pages 103 through 122.

CHAPTER 10
Growth Through Reading

On Prayer

Parker, Dr. William, & Elaine St. Johns, *Prayer Can Change Your Life* (Prentice Hall)

Olson, Kermit, *First Steps in Prayer* (Revell)

Rinker, Rosalind. *Communicating Love Through Prayer, Praying Together,* (Zondervan) *Teaching Conversational Prayer* (Word).

Pert, George & Florence, *Get Going Through Small Groups* (Guideposts, Carmel, N.Y. 10512) — $1.00.

Reprints: from *His* magazine. *Conversational Prayer.* 25 for $4.00. Order from: Reprints, 4605 Sherwood, Downers Grove, Ill. 60515. Prepaid only: make check to: *His* Reprints.

On Daily Devotions

Scripture Union Bible study. P.O. Box 269, Upper Darby, Pa. 19084. Quarterly study notes for various ages. Samples sent on request.

Oswald Chambers. *My Utmost for His Highest* (Dodd-Mead)

Search the Scriptures (Inter-Varsity Press) Through the Bible in three years of daily readings. Excellent for advanced study. Box F, Downers Grove, Ill. 60515

God Calling, A Devotional Diary, edited by A. J. Russell, (Dodd, Mead & Co.).

On Jesus Christ
  Bickersteth, Edward, *The Trinity* (Kregel)
  Carnegie-Simpson, P. *The Fact of Christ,* (Inter-Varsity Press)
  Phillips, J.B. *Is God at Home?* (Abingdon)
  — When God Became Man, (Abingdon)
  Nelson, Wesley, *Captivated by Christ* (C.L.C.)
  Rinker, Rosalind, *Who Is This Man?* (Zondervan)
    (Study in Mark: to reveal the living Christ among us)

CHAPTER 11

How This Book Has
Helped Others

Things people learned, upon their first experience with Conversational Prayer:

>The importance of things.
>the simpleness of prayer.
>barriers are gone between us.
>others have similar problems:
>God is not away out yonder, but here.
>I prayed about things I didn't even
>   know were wrong with me!
>I felt I belonged.
>it made me feel others cared about me.

Teens tell why they like Conversational Prayer. After a Workshop on Prayer, they were instructed to stand in groups of four, and follow the Four Basic steps as given on page 87.

>Really great!
>New experience.
>Wow! Wow! Wow! It gave us a lift!
>It hit home.
>Never thought of prayer like this.

I'd like to do it again.
Different. Workable.
Good for us, but it was hard.
We faced reality.
I was close to tears all the time.
First time I ever felt God present.
It made you feel loved.
I had never done anything like this before.
It was a cool idea!
It was groovy! It made you feel like you could talk
    about anything and everyone would understand.
Out of sight! Something every church group should do.
It makes a person feel he's important in this world,
    and that everyone can have a purpose.

The excerpts below are from unsolicited letters of testimony to
the effectiveness of this book on Prayer. These have been selected
from a great number of letters received by the author.

Dear Ros,
    Tonight I must try to express my gratitude for your books. All
too often I read a book and am helped by its message but fail
to acknowledge that fact to the author.
    Many years ago as a teenager at a church camp where I was
"kitchen help" I found your book, Prayer — Conversing With God,
on top of the fridge. I spent the better part of an afternoon de-
vouring it. From that point on I read everything of yours I could
get my hands on. I give your books away as Christmas gifts.
    I attended the IVCF Urbana Conference, and found the Bible
study and prayer groups the most valuable part of the conference,
so upon returning home I started such a group. At that time I
was able to put into practice many of your suggestions.
    I am an R.N.A. (Registered Nursing Assistant) and find many
of my patients enjoy your books. Some of my friends are Roman
Catholic nuns — sharing your books with them has brought much
joy and many precious hours.